LEGENDS OF FLIGHT

DOUGLAS
DC-3

A Legends of Flight Illustrated History

WOLFGANG BORGMANN

SCHIFFER MILITARY
4880 Lower Valley Road Atglen, PA 19310

Dedication

For Tom Weihe

Other Schiffer books by the author
Boeing 707: A Legends of Flight Illustrated History, 978-0-7643-6345-0
McDonnell Douglas DC-10/MD-11: A Legends of Flight Illustrated History, 978-0-7643-6137-1

Other Schiffer books on related subjects
Boeing 727: Triumph in the Skies, Dan Dornseif, 978-0-7643-6051-0
Boeing Metamorphosis: Launching the 737 and 747, 1965–69, John Fredrickson with John Andrew, 978-0-7643-6162-3

Cover design by Molly Shields
Type set in DIN Alternate/Minion Pro

ISBN: 978-0-7643-6710-6
Printed in India

Published by Schiffer Publishing, Ltd.
4880 Lower Valley Road
Atglen, PA 19310
Phone: (610) 593-1777; Fax: (610) 593-2002
Email: Info@schifferbooks.com
Web: www.schifferbooks.com

For our complete selection of fine books on this and related subjects, please visit our website at www.schifferbooks.com. You may also write for a free catalog.

Schiffer Publishing's titles are available at special discounts for bulk purchases for sales promotions or premiums. Special editions, including personalized covers, corporate imprints, and excerpts, can be created in large quantities for special needs. For more information, contact the publisher.

We are always looking for people to write books on new and related subjects. If you have an idea for a book, please contact us at proposals@schifferbooks.com.

FSC
www.fsc.org
MIX
Paper from responsible sources
FSC® C016779

CONTENTS

FOREWORD

When I was asked to write a book about the DC-3, several thoughts immediately popped into my head. First, there was the great anticipation of enriching the Legends of Flight series with a volume about *the* aviation legend par excellence. No series of books about the most-significant airliners of all time could fail to include one about the DC-3. But this immediately raised a question: What does one write about a legend of aviation about which everything has already been written and said? After much pondering, figure skating came to mind. What does that have to do with the Douglas DC-3, you might well ask, dear reader? The answer is quite simple: in competitive ice skating, there is the compulsory part of the competition with prescribed figures—in the case of this book, the description of the development history of the DC-3 and its technical specifications—and the freestyle part of the competition with special jumps and other maneuvers. In a figurative sense, these are the civilian and military operations described in this book. Their selection, I must admit, in a book like this with its limited scope, can only be purely subjective and brief. Much more could be said and written about the DC-3 and C-47—and some readers may miss this and that detail, for which I ask for understanding at this point.

As is well known, the DC-3 and its military versions were used around the globe by various militaries and just about every Western airline of the time. This aircraft type saw service in almost every country in the world, including the USSR. Its basic design goes back to the Douglas Commercial 1, or DC-1 for short, of 1933, whose development was initiated by the president of Transcontinental & Western Air (TWA), Jack Frye. For decades, the common saying was "the best replacement for a DC-3 is a DC-3." Countless aircraft manufacturers tried with varying degrees of success to build a successor to the indestructible Douglas. This resulted in a few bestsellers such as the Fokker F-27 Friendship, but also in designs that were never sold in large numbers, such as the Handley Page Herald or SAAB 90 Scandia. The fact that the Super DC-3 offered by Douglas after the end of the Second World War was a flop shows that the DC-3 design is best as it was first launched on December 17, 1935. Improved versions failed to convince either the armed forces or the airlines, which held on to their C-47s and DC-3s. The only exception was the US Navy's R4D-8 (C-117D), developed from the Super DC-3. The design of a DC-5 with parameters closely resembling those of the DC-3 was also doomed

The British airline Air Atlantique was still operating Douglas DC-3s on commercial passenger, cargo, and pollution control flights in Europe in the 1990s. *Air Atlantique*

The airline's DC-3s were used to monitor British coastal waters in order to quickly detect environmental pollution from the air—and to remove dangerous oil slicks by dropping chemical substances. The DC-3s were stationed in Coventry, where this photo was taken in 1998. *Author's photo*

to failure. Basler Turbo Conversions, based at the aviation mecca of Oshkosh, Wisconsin, brought the DC-3 into the twenty-first century with its turboprop conversions of these historic aircraft. The fact that the German research station at the South Pole can rely on that Basler BT-67 for transport in the perpetual ice confirms the initially curious concept of combining a thoroughly overhauled vintage aircraft structure with a new engine to create a transport aircraft with future potential.

Why the DC-1 was built, what improvements went into the DC-2, what role TWA and American Airlines played in the development of the first Douglas Commercial models—all this falls under the heading of "compulsory" in my allegory. Under the heading "freestyle," however, this book offers much more. First of all, there is the presentation of the aircraft types with which the Douglas twins were competing at the time of their first flights, such as the Boeing 247, and what distinguished them from those types. The Dutch airline KLM took part in a very special air race from London to Melbourne, Australia, in 1934, entering a DC-2 with the name "Uiver" (Stork). In the process, Douglas demonstrated the outstanding design that would ultimately lead to the DC-3. The potential of the aircraft, christened

the Skytrain by the US Army Air Corps and the Dakota by the British, became the Allies' standard transport aircraft, flying countless missions during World War II. Together with the larger, four-engine Douglas DC-4, it made a decisive contribution to the Allied victory. The role the C-47 played in aid deliveries by the British and American governments to the Chinese government of Chiang Kai-Shek, which was cut off by Japanese troops, and what the aircraft accomplished on these China National Aviation Corporation (CAAC) missions over the Himalayas between 1942 and 1945, is described in the chapter "The Hump." The Berlin Airlift in 1948 and 1949 was a humanitarian-aid airlift that remains unique to this day. In particular, this book outlines the role played by the Dakotas of the Royal Air Force as well as a variety of civilian airlines that were instrumental in the success of the airlift.

After the end of World War II, Germans were forbidden to fly or operate their own airline from 1945 until 1955, when the newly founded Lufthansa took off. What many people don't know is that it was not an Allied airline that filled this gap for ten years, but the Scandinavian Airlines System (SAS). With its Douglas DC-3s in particular, it maintained a dense domestic German network, initially limited to the Western Allied zones and, from 1949, to the new Federal Republic of Germany. This book describes the background and operational details of SAS's unusual, unofficial status as the "national carrier" of West Germany.

That and much more are part of this edition of the Legends of Flight series devoted entirely to the Dakota, Gooney Bird, and Skytrain.

Wolfgang Borgmann
Oerlinghausen, spring 2022

In South Africa, DC-3s flew for the state-owned South African Airways (SAA), among others. Their passengers were transported to the aircraft by what today appear to be antiquated apron buses. *Transnet*

"Daisy," the DC-3 owned by the Swedish Flying Veterans Association, on the ramp, its metal skin shimmering in the sunlight. Its livery corresponds to that of Scandinavian Airlines in the 1950s. *Author's photo*

Bottom left: Conscientious maintenance was also important in the pioneering years of air travel. Here, a DC-3 of the German vacation airline Bavaria being serviced by Lufthansa's technical department at Hamburg. *Hamburg Airport*

Below: The DC-3, "Clipper Tabitha May," registered N33611, has been painted in vintage Pan American–PAA colors. *Author's photo*

In the early postwar years, carriage of air freight and mail was one of the main sources of income for the Swedish airline AB Aerotransport (ABA), which issued this postcard at the time. *Author's collection*

This photo from the late 1940s illustrates the considerable size difference between the DC-3 and the Boeing 377 Stratocruiser, then the largest and most luxurious airliner on Pan American Airways' long-range route network. *Boeing*

There is almost no country on the earth in which the Douglas DC-3 did not see service in its wide array of versions and in some cases still does to this day. One such country is Canada. This photo depicts one such aircraft in the colors of Canadian Pacific Airlines (CP Air), which operated from 1942 to 1987. *Sören Nielsen via Tom Weihe*

In 2007, the author was involved in organizing the Hamburg Airport Days air show, and, among other things, he invited all of the Douglas DC-3s flying in Europe to this event. The result was this photo of the static display area, in which nine Skytrains/Dakotas can be made out. *Hamburg Airport, Michael Penner*

Hollywood stars took Pan Am's long-range flights to Frankfurt/Main, and from there traveled on to their European engagements by DC-3. *Dr. John Provan*

Like this DC-3 stewardess of the Swedish airline
ABA-SILA in the 1940s, I hope that you enjoy your
flight through the history of the immortal
Douglas DC-3! *Mats Alfvåg*

CHAPTER 1
THE BIRTH OF A LEGEND

On December 17, 1935, the first Douglas DC-3 took off from Santa Monica, California, on its maiden flight. The impetus for the development of modern commercial aircraft by the Douglas Aircraft Company came from a competing product from Seattle. The twin-engine Boeing 247 was one of the most advanced and fastest airliners of its time, but Boeing managers made a fatal marketing mistake that they were to regret for a long time to come.

TWA was founded on October 1, 1930, from the merger of Standard Airlines, Maddux Air Lines, Western Air Express (WAE), and Transcontinental Air Transport (TAT) to form Transcontinental & Western Air. It was not until May 17, 1950, that management changed the name to Trans World Airlines, by which it was known until its acquisition by American Airlines in 2001. Jack Frye was vice president of operations at the time of the company's founding and was named president of the fledgling airline in 1934. Together with Paul E. Richter and Walter A. Hamilton, Frye determined the airline's fortunes for many years. In addition to the DC-1, the triumvirate also initiated construction of the DC-2, the Boeing 307 Stratoliner, and the Lockheed Constellation. The three senior TWA managers were joined by Tommy Tomlinson, who, along with Atlantic pioneer Charles Lindbergh, Jack Frye, and TWA's first president, Richard W. Robinson, formed

The only example of the Douglas DC-1 that was built, photographed in front of Glendale Airport's art-deco-style terminal in California. *Douglas / Ron Handgraaf*

TWA's technical committee at its New York headquarters. One of the team's first tasks was to investigate several crashes involving the Fokker F-10 trimotors that TWA operated on its transcontinental flights. It quickly became apparent that the type's wooden wings had failed in flight—moisture had likely penetrated and softened the structure in an area not visible during routine inspections. As a result, TWA grounded its entire fleet of Fokker F-10s and scrambled to find a replacement. But suitable alternatives were simply not available—or were out of reach for TWA.

Left: The Langley Research Center tested this navy Douglas R2D-1 at its testing facility in Hampton, Virginia. R2D-1 was the navy designation for the DC-2, which was used by the US Navy and Marine Corps to carry passengers and freight. *NASA*

Below: The Dutch airline KLM was an important customer for the DC-2. Anthony Fokker acquired the marketing rights for the aircraft in Europe from Douglas. *KLM*

Douglas Aircraft Company advertising brochure for the first two versions of their best-seller—the Douglas Sleeper Transport (DST) and the DC-3. *Douglas / Ron Handgraaf*

The DST-144 "Sky Sleeper" with the registration NC16002 pictured here took off on its maiden flight in 1936 as construction number 1496 and was lost in a crash on December 28, 1948. All thirty-two occupants of the aircraft, which was operated by Airborne Transport at the time, were killed. *Douglas / Ron Handgraaf*

American Airlines was the first customer for the Douglas Sleeper Transport—and thus the DC-3. *Douglas / Ron Handgraaf*

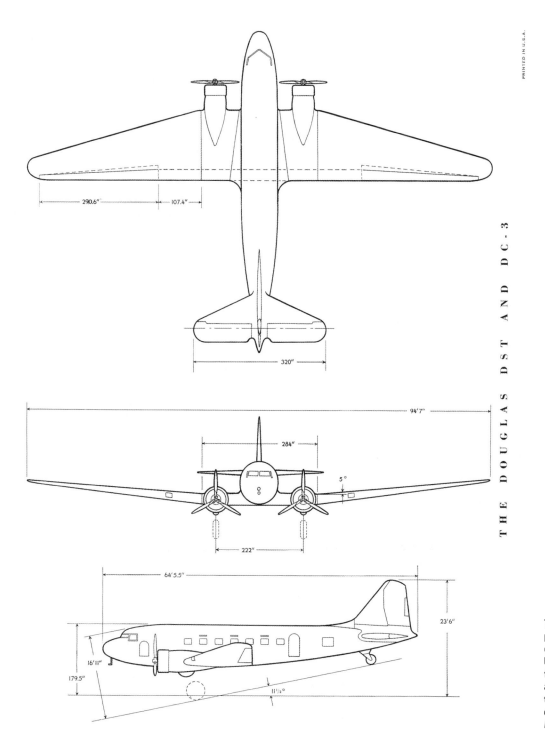

THE DOUGLAS DST AND DC-3

This three-view drawing published by Douglas shows not only the dimensions of the DST, but also the type's special features in the form of additional windows compared to the DC-3, which had been conceived for day flights.
Douglas / Ron Handgraaf

EQUIPMENT

Pilots' Compartment

Fuel Pressure Gauges (2)
Oil Pressure Gauges (2)
Rate of Climb Indicator
Turn and Bank Indicator
Turn and Bank Venturi
Airspeed Indicator (1—Provision for 2)
Pitot Static Tube (1—Provision for 2)
Clocks (2)
Fuel Pressure Switches (2)
Oil Pressure Switches (2)
Compass
Sensitive Altimeters (2)
Manifold Pressure Gauges (2)
Carburetor Air Temperature Indicators (2)
Oil Temperature Indicators (2)
Outside Air Temperature Indicator
Tachometers (2)
Engine Temperature Indicators (2)
Voltammeters (2)
Vacuum Relief Valve
Synchroscope
Fuel Quantity Gauge
Voltage Compensator

Power Plant

Hamilton Standard Three-Blade Hydro-Controllable Constant-Speed Propellers (2)
Hamilton Standard Constant-Speed Governors (2)
Fuel Pumps (2)
Oil Coolers (2)
Automatic Oil Temperature Regulators (2)
Direct Hand Electric Engine Starters (2)

Electrical

Landing Gear Signal Horn
85 Ampere Battery (1—Provision for 2)
Landing Lights (2)
Passing Light
Complete Radio Shielding
Generator (1—Provision for 2)
Running Lights (2)
Tail Light

Lavatory

Toilets (2—DST, 1—DC-3)
Wash Basins (2—DST, 1—DC-3)
Mirrors (2—DST, 1—DC-3)
Toilet Paper Holders (2—DST, 1—DC-3)
Towel Holders (2—DST, 1—DC-3)

Kotex Dispenser
Kleenex Dispenser
Paper Cup Dispensers (2—DST, 1—DC-3)
Paper Cup Waste Container (2—DST, 1—DC-3)
Thermos Bottles (2)
Seat with Cushion (DC-3), Bench with Cushion (DST)
Safety Belts for all Fixed Seats and Stewardess' Seat
Holder for Toilet Chemical

Galley

Food Compartment
Utility Compartment
Serving Trays (2—DST, 21—DC-3)
Thermos Bottles (8—DST, 12—DC-3)
Hot Food Containers (5—DST)

Miscellaneous

Automatic Pilot
Two-Engine CO$_2$ Pressure Fire Extinguisher System
Hand Fire Extinguishers (2)
Parachute Flares (2)
Combined Log Book Container
Map Case
First Aid Kit and Holder
Flash Light Holders (2)
Cabin Seat Belt Signs (In Each Compartment—DST, 1—DC-3)
Ash Trays, Cabin (7—DST, 14—DC-3) Pilots' Compartment (2)
DST Dressing Rooms (1 each)
Removable Tables (4—DST only)
Air Sickness Holders and Containers (14—DST, 24—DC-3)
Hat Clips (2—DST, 34—DC-3)
Literature Pockets
Down Mattresses (7—DST only, for upper berths)
Down Mattresses (7—DST only, for lower berths)
Baggage Straps (10—DST, 15—DC-3)

Special Equipment—Extra Charge

Provision is made for the installation of Western Electric Model 208-D Radio Equipment.
The Transport may be equipped with De-Icer for wings, tail surfaces and propellers.
Alcoholic De-Icer system is available for propellers, carburetors and windshield.
Pillows, sheets and blankets.

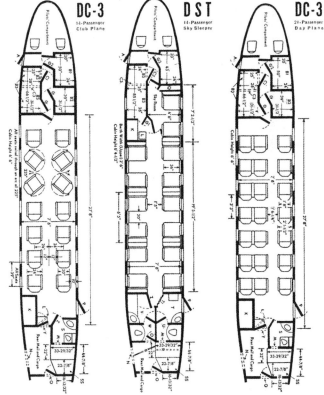

A —External Cargo Loading Door 22" W. x 35" H.
B1—No. 1 Front Righthand Mail and Cargo
B2—No. 2 Front Righthand Mail and Cargo
B3—Front Lefthand Mail and Cargo
C1—Cargo Doors 21½" W. x 29" H.
C2—Cargo Door 21½" W. x 31" H.
C3—Opening through partition 28" W. x 30" H.
G —Cargo Doors 19" W. x 49" H.
G1—Cargo Door 17" W. x 68" H.
G2—Cargo Door 21" W. x 42" H.
K —Galley
L —Folding Stewardess' Seat
M—Door opening downward to rear cargo 19" W. x 20⅞" H.

N —Baggage Loading Door 28" W. x 24" H., opens upward
O —Rear Baggage Doors, 21" W. x 38½" H.
P —Main Entry Door 28" W. x 60" H.
Q —Coat Closet
R —Clothes Rail
S —Lavatory
SS—Auxiliary Shelf 44" average height from floor
T —Men's Dressing Room
T1—Dressing Room Curtain
U —Men's Lavatory
V —Ladies' Lounge
W—Ladies' Lavatory
Y —Door to Baggage 21" W. x 50" H.
Z —Lavatory Door

These drawings illustrate the different cabin configurations for the DC-3 and DST for day and night flights. *Douglas / Ron Handgraaf*

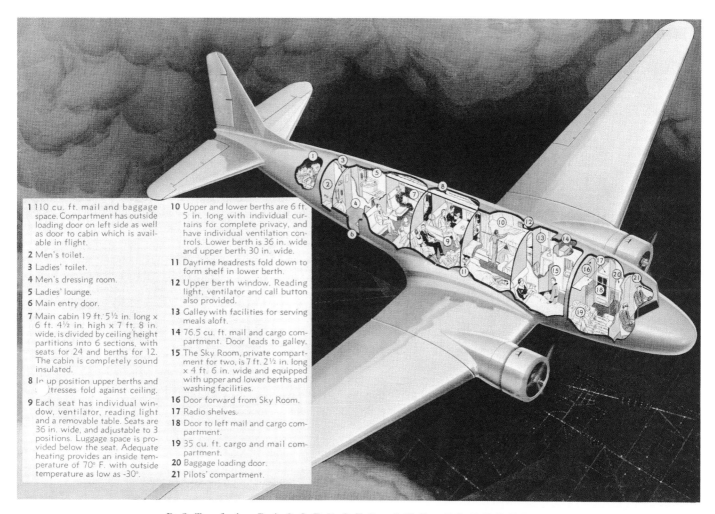

1 110 cu. ft. mail and baggage space. Compartment has outside loading door on left side as well as door to cabin which is available in flight.

2 Men's toilet.

3 Ladies' toilet.

4 Men's dressing room.

5 Ladies' lounge.

6 Main entry door.

7 Main cabin 19 ft. 5½ in. long x 6 ft. 4½ in. high x 7 ft. 8 in. wide, is divided by ceiling height partitions into 6 sections, with seats for 24 and berths for 12. The cabin is completely sound insulated.

8 In up position upper berths and mattresses fold against ceiling.

9 Each seat has individual window, ventilator, reading light and a removable table. Seats are 36 in. wide, and adjustable to 3 positions. Luggage space is provided below the seat. Adequate heating provides an inside temperature of 70° F. with outside temperature as low as -30°.

10 Upper and lower berths are 6 ft. 5 in. long with individual curtains for complete privacy, and have individual ventilation controls. Lower berth is 36 in. wide and upper berth 30 in. wide.

11 Daytime headrests fold down to form shelf in lower berth.

12 Upper berth window. Reading light, ventilator and call button also provided.

13 Galley with facilities for serving meals aloft.

14 76.5 cu. ft. mail and cargo compartment. Door leads to galley.

15 The Sky Room, private compartment for two, is 7 ft. 2½ in. long x 4 ft. 6 in. wide and equipped with upper and lower berths and washing facilities.

16 Door forward from Sky Room.

17 Radio shelves.

18 Door to left mail and cargo compartment.

19 35 cu. ft. cargo and mail compartment.

20 Baggage loading door.

21 Pilots' compartment.

DST 14-PASSENGER SKY SLEEPER

5

A view of the cabin of the DST "Sky Sleeper," illustrating the cabin configuration for fourteen passengers on night flights. *Douglas / Ron Handgraaf*

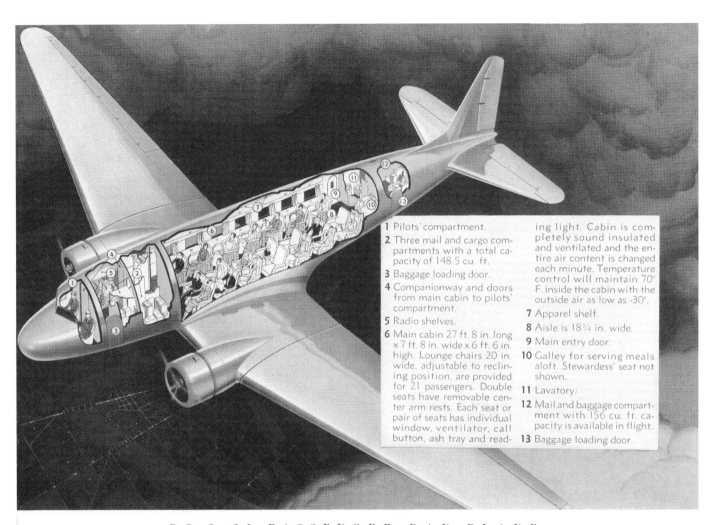

1 Pilots' compartment.

2 Three mail and cargo compartments with a total capacity of 148.5 cu. ft.

3 Baggage loading door.

4 Companionway and doors from main cabin to pilots' compartment.

5 Radio shelves.

6 Main cabin 27 ft. 8 in. long x 7 ft. 8 in. wide x 6 ft. 6 in. high. Lounge chairs 20 in. wide, adjustable to reclining position, are provided for 21 passengers. Double seats have removable center arm rests. Each seat or pair of seats has individual window, ventilator, call button, ash tray and reading light. Cabin is completely sound insulated and ventilated and the entire air content is changed each minute. Temperature control will maintain 70° F. inside the cabin with the outside air as low as -30°.

7 Apparel shelf.

8 Aisle is 18¼ in. wide.

9 Main entry door.

10 Galley for serving meals aloft. Stewardess' seat not shown.

11 Lavatory.

12 Mail and baggage compartment with 156 cu. ft. capacity is available in flight.

13 Baggage loading door.

DC-3 21-PASSENGER DAY PLANE

7

In comparison, this drawing illustrates the DC-3's cabin configured for day flights with seats for twenty-one passengers. *Douglas / Ron Handgraaf*

Above: A view of the interior of a Douglas Sleeper Transport.
Douglas / Ron Handgraaf

Left: The cockpit of one of the first Douglas DC-3s to be built.
Douglas / Ron Handgraaf

The latter category included the Boeing 247, for which United Air Lines placed an order in 1932 for sixty Boeing 247D aircraft with seating capacity for ten passengers. Compared with the basic model, the D version featured various design improvements such as variable-pitch propellers, low-drag engine cowlings, and rear-facing cockpit windows. Another novelty: the B 247 was the first twin-engine, low-wing commercial aircraft to be able to maintain altitude with a full payload on a single engine. Maximum seating capacity was ten passengers, who were seated in individual armchairs with armrests, with the seats separated by a comfortable distance of about 3 feet. A galley, from which guests were served by a stewardess, was located in the rear of the squat cabin. Transcontinental and Western Air (TWA) was also interested in the new aircraft from Seattle, but Boeing managers had reserved the first sixty Model 247s for United. Boeing was unwilling to provide aircraft to

Backs of the seats in the DST are removable, and . . .

are inserted between the seats to form the lower berth.

The upper berth, with mattress, lets down from ceiling.

Adjustable seats in the 21-Passenger DC-3 afford comfort to persons of small or large stature. Seat backs normally recline 15° and may be lowered 30° farther.

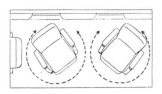

Seats in the Club Plane swivel through an arc of 225°.

Left: This drawing explains the adjustable seats of the DC-3 and DST versions. *Douglas / Ron Handgraaf*

Above: The cabin of a DST, which can be identified by the small windows in the upper fuselage area, prior to installation of the cabin interior. *Douglas / Ron Handgraaf*

TWA until it had delivered the last aircraft to United. So, of necessity, the TWA technical committee went in search of alternatives. This began with a legendary letter sent by Jack Frye to selected American aircraft manufacturers on August 2, 1932. All the letters contained the identical wording: "Transcontinental & Western Air is interested in purchasing ten or more trimotored transport planes. I am attaching our general performance specifications covering this equipment, and would appreciate your advising whether your company is interested in this manufacturing job. If so, approximately how long would it take to turn out the first plane for service tests?"

KLM provided service to South Africa with its DC-3s. This photo was taken at Johannesburg Airport. *Transnet*

The attachment further stated, "Please consider this information confidential and return specifications if you are not interested."

This letter had been preceded by heated discussions in the TWA Technical Committee about the number of engines required to meet TWA pilots' demand for a safe flight from Winslow, Arizona, over the high country to Albuquerque, New Mexico—even with one engine out. The specifications also included a requirement for "satisfactory takeoffs under good control at any TWA airport on any combination of two engines." In addition, the aircraft was to be able to carry at least twelve passengers in comfortable seats with ample space

"and have a 1,080-mile range at 150 mph and a one-engine-out service ceiling of 10,000 feet." Fry received prompt responses from the three manufacturers—General Aviation, the successor to Fokker, Douglas, and Sikorsky. With the exception of Douglas, which proposed a twin, all the other proposals were three-engine designs similar to the earlier Fokker aircraft and the Ford Trimotor. Tommy Tomlinson's task was to review the submitted papers in terms of the required performance parameters, but the discussion in the Technical Committee continued unabated as to whether it had to be a trimotor—or if it could be a twin. Finally, it was concluded that the Sikorsky proposal was unsuitable and that Douglas and General Aviation should be encouraged to build prototypes so that the aircraft could be selected as the result of direct comparison. It quickly became apparent that General Aviation's design would be much more expensive than predicted, and North American Aviation, to which General Aviation now belonged, decided to abandon the project in the early summer of 1933 and scrap the prototype that was under construction. What remained was the Douglas DC-1—the forebearer of the legendary DC-2 and DC-3 aircraft family, of which more than 12,000 were to be built. The prototype flew for the first time on July 1, 1933.

The DC-1's modern design, which incorporated numerous innovations in aircraft construction, offered not only a more spacious passenger cabin, but also far better flight performance than the Boeing 247, of which just seventy-five were sold. On February 18, 1934, a TWA DC-1 set a new speed record between the East and West Coasts of the United States. At the controls were Jack Frye and legendary pilot Eddie Rickenbacker, and the DC-1 carried six bags of mail from Burbank, California, to Newark on the US East Coast in thirteen hours and four minutes. Even faster was a TWA DC-1 crew on April 30, 1935, which covered the distance between Los Angeles and New York in eleven hours and five minutes.

Enthused by this potential, TWA ordered the larger DC-2 production version with 720 hp engines. At first glance almost a twin of the DC-1, the DC-2 differed from its predecessor in having a longer fuselage and improved performance. TWA took delivery of the first one on May 13, 1934, and put it into service on the Newark–Chicago route just five days later. On August 1 of that year, TWA inaugurated its Sky Chief service with its DC-2s, departing Newark at four in the afternoon and landing in Los Angeles at seven the next day. This first night service across the continental United States was a sensation in 1934! One hundred fifty-six examples of this initial version of the original Douglas propeller-driven airliner were produced and flew with airlines in the United States, Asia, and Europe. The Dutch aircraft manufacturer Anthony Fokker was so enthusiastic about the DC-2 that he acquired the European sales rights for the type. Fokker's first customer was the Dutch airline KLM, which operated its DC-2 on scheduled flights from Amsterdam to the Dutch East Indies—today's Indonesia. A KLM DC-2 achieved world fame in the MacRobertson Air Race, which took it from London to Melbourne, Australia, in October 1934. The Dutch crew, with German aviation journalist Thea Rasche on board, reached the finish line after ninety hours and was the winner in the commercial aircraft category.

In 1934, the Dutch airline KLM took part in the legendary MacRobertson Trophy Air Race between the British capital of London and Melbourne, Australia, entering its DC-2 "Uiver" (stork). *Author's photo*

The livery of the new "Uiver" is a perfect copy of the historic PH-AJU. *Author's photo*

THEA RASCHE: THE "FLYING FRÄULEIN"

THE KLM DC-2 UIVER (STORK) ACHIEVES WORLD FAME

Thea Rasche was a student of aviation pioneer Paul Bäumer at Hamburg-Fuhlsbüttel, learned to fly with him in 1925, and shortly thereafter became the first German female pilot to obtain an aerobatic license. In 1927, she toured the United States in her own Udet U12 Flamingo and soon became famous as the "Flying Fräulein." In 1929 she was accepted into the prestigious Ninety-Nines. This international association of women pilots had been founded by the legendary American aviatrix Amelia Earhart, who disappeared without a trace in her plane over the Pacific Ocean in 1937. During this adventurous time in the United States, Rasche met other aviation icons such as Charles Lindbergh as well as the polar aviator Bernt Balchen.

In 1934, Thea Rasche had been working for a year as editor in chief of the weekly magazine *Deutsche Flugillustrierte* (German Flight Illustrated) in Berlin, and she used her contacts with the Dutch airline KLM to take part in the legendary MacRobertson Air Race between England and Melbourne, Australia, which remains the largest of its kind to this day, aboard the airline's Douglas DC-2 PH-AJU Uiver (Stork). This air race, which took place in October and November and involved some twenty

Bottom left: Officially booked as a KLM passenger, Thea Rasche traveled with this ticket on the record-breaking flight from London to Melbourne. This was also the first flight by a modern all-metal commercial aircraft from Europe to Australia. *Noel Jackling*

Below: German aviation journalist Thea Rasche posing with "Uiver's" two Dutch pilots, Moll and Parmentier. *Noel Jackling*

aircraft in various categories, was organized to mark the 100th birthday of the Australian state of Victoria and its capital, Melbourne. The race began at Mildenhall, and the participating aircraft took off at forty-five-second intervals. Contemporaneous reports said that Rasche planned to take part in this air race herself, flying a Messerschmitt Bf 108 Taifun, but Germany's Nazi government refused to allow her to participate since it believed she stood no chance of winning.

Thea Rasche, whose mother held a Dutch passport, was the only female reporter flying in one of the participating aircraft, and she submitted enthusiastic reports from the Uiver. In this way, she inspired millions of people around the globe, who eagerly followed her heartfelt accounts in the world's major daily newspapers. After arriving in Australia, Thea Rasche immediately traveled on to the United States. There she was celebrated as if she had piloted the DC-2 herself. One honor followed the next—and the American first lady Eleanor Roosevelt even received Paul Bäumer's former flight student at the White House!

After her return to Germany, the Nazi regime "rewarded" Rasche's commitment to understanding between peoples by dismissing her as editor in chief of the *Deutsche Flugillustrierte*. During World War II, Rasche refused to give propaganda speeches for the Third Reich or to work as a ferry pilot, which violated her ideals of friendship among nations through aviation. She died impoverished in 1971.

THEA RASCHE ON HER PARTICIPATION IN THE MACROBERTSON AIR RACE

"The MacRobertson race was really my greatest experience. Not only the abundance of new impressions, but the inner experience, the feeling of togetherness and solidarity among the aviators of the various nations, the helpfulness at every place we flew into, the will to understand, the open hearts everywhere—that was the overwhelming thing that can hardly be put into words.—To be an aviator means to be a comrade, means to be victorious over time and distances!"

Aviation journalist Thea Rasche reported live from the MacRobertson Air Race for an audience of millions around the globe. Here she photographs the mayor of the Australian town of Albury, where "Uiver" had been obliged to make an emergency landing at night about 180 miles short of its destination in Melbourne. The DC-2 had been caught in a thunderstorm with freezing rain, and the crew became completely disoriented. Mayor Alfred Waugh came to the rescue, turning the street lights of Albury on and off to signal the name of the town in Morse code, which was recognized by the DC-2 crew circling overhead. He also ordered the townspeople to use their cars to illuminate the town's racetrack, which had been converted into a makeshift airstrip—thus enabling the crew to make an emergency landing. All went well, and the DC-2 was able to safely fly on to Melbourne and victory in the commercial aircraft category the following morning. *Noel Jackling*

After a safe landing in Melbourne, "Uiver's" three passengers pose for the camera: Piet Gilissen (*far left*), Roelof Domenie (*right*), and Thea Rasche. With them is Alfred Waugh, the mayor of the Australian town of Albury. Thea Rasche and Roelof Domenie are wearing their MacRobertson Air Race gold medals. *Noel Jackling*

Thea Rasche and her initial flight instructor and close friend Paul Bäumer, waving the flag of the German Free and Hanseatic City of Hamburg. *Author's archive*

THE AVIODOME MUSEUM'S NEW UIVER (STORK)

The Dutch aviation museum Aviodome acquired a DC-2 to commemorate the air race from London to Melbourne and KLM Royal Dutch Airlines' participation with its new Uiver (Stork). The choice fell on construction number 1404, produced in 1935, which was initially delivered by Douglas to the US Navy on September 7 of that year. After an eventful life, in the early 1990s this rare airliner was owned by an American multimillionaire named Colgate W. Darden III. The Aviodome Museum and Darden eventually came to an agreement, and the DC-2 changed hands. In the summer of 1999, the new pride of the Dutch aviation museum reached European soil after a ferry flight across the North Atlantic. It is the last airworthy Douglas DC-2 anywhere in the world, but it is currently on display at the museum, painted in the historical colors that it wore during the air race to Melbourne.

If TWA had been able to acquire the Boeing 247 at shorter notice and production of the DC-1 had not taken place, commercial aviation would initially have taken a different path. What this would have looked like, and what the competing Boeing offered its airlines and passengers, is described in a Lufthansa report from 1934.

At the time of the Boeing order, the German airline, founded in 1926, had no comparable twin-engine aircraft. Neither the Junkers Ju 86 nor the Heinkel He 111 became available until 1935–36. On April 1, 1934, Lufthansa let the public know that "in the course of developing and procuring further first-class aircraft for German aviation, a number of commercial aircraft have also been purchased in the United States." Lufthansa continued, "After it became known that the American Boeing 247 airliner was being used in larger numbers on transcontinental routes in the United States, Lufthansa decided to purchase three aircraft of this type from United Aircraft Export Inc." In addition to using them in regular air service, the Reich Aviation Ministry also hoped "to be able to compare in practice the aircraft used in Germany with one of the best aircraft types built in the United States." While construction numbers 1944 and 1945 arrived in Germany in the spring of 1934, the Boeing 247 with construction number 1946 was used for flight tests in Seattle in September 1934 but was never accepted by Lufthansa. Prior to delivery of the two aircraft with the American registrations NC90Y and NC91Y, which were given the German registrations D-AGAR and D-AKIN, extensive flight testing was carried out at Boeing Field in Seattle under the supervision of Lufthansa's then chief engineer, Dr. Erich Schatzki.

Line up of Dakota Norway DC-3 (*front*), DC-2 "Uiver," and Lisunov Li-2 at the Hamburg Airport Days air show in 2007. *Author's photo*

The German airline Lufthansa operated two brand-new Boeing 247D airliners in 1934 and 1935. The aircraft had been disassembled in Seattle and shipped to Germany by sea. *Lufthansa*

LUFTHANSA TESTS THE BOEING 247

Safely packed in shipping crates, the two Boeing aircraft arrived by sea in Germany, where they were immediately assembled. Lufthansa tested them "thoroughly," as evidenced by the *Report on the Testing of the Boeing Mod. 247 W-No. 1945 D-AGAR*, issued by the airline's Technical Development Department on August 18, 1934. The airframe, engine, electrical system, and onboard equipment all were examined in detail. The technical analysis, including numerous detailed photographs, concluded: "In summary, it can be said that the design of the Boeing Model 247 is practical. . . . The shop work, especially the finish of the smooth sheet

metal[,] is very neat. For German aircraft construction, the machine offers much that is new." Aircraft D-AGAR served on Lufthansa's European route network in 1934 and 1935; however, it sustained irreparable damage in a collision with an Air France aircraft at Nuremberg Airport. D-AKIN continued to fly for two more years, but in 1937 it crashed during a test flight, ending this first chapter in the history of Boeing and Lufthansa. Lufthansa's first Boeing 707 arrived at Hamburg on March 2, 1960, opening not only a new chapter for the German airline—but also a new age in air transport.

The layout of the Boeing 247D's cockpit was very modern for its time. *Lufthansa*

THE DC-1 SETS NEW STANDARDS

Aviation history took a different course, however, and on September 20, 1932, some two months after Frye's letter to the American aircraft manufacturers, TWA and Douglas signed a purchase agreement, initially for one DC-1. TWA's demand that the aircraft be able to take off and reach its destination safely on just one engine, long before this was required by the certification authority, and Douglas's response in the form of the DC-1 show not only the airline's foresight but also the quality of the aircraft design. Just four months after its maiden flight with Carol Cover and Edmund T. "Eddie" Allen at the controls, the Douglas Commercial One received its type certificate. The first flight almost ended in disaster after the aircraft's engines failed one after another as it climbed. Only an emergency landing on a nearby golf course prevented the worst. The cause was discovered only after three more flights, all of which frightened observers: the carburetors had been installed upside down, and this was not noticed when the engines were assembled. With its twin 710 hp Wright Cyclone radial engines, the DC-1 could carry twelve passengers—two more than the competing Boeing 247. The DC-1 was also faster and had a longer range than its archrival. The launch customer, TWA, set a speed record on February 19, 1934, when the DC-1 flew between the East and West Coasts of the United States. The airline ordered twenty examples of the DC-2, the production version of the DC-1, which had been lengthened by 18 inches and equipped with 720 hp engines. The first TWA aircraft entered regular service on May 18, 1934, on the Columbus–Pittsburgh–New York route and, with its fourteen seats instead of the DC-1's twelve, brought extra revenue potential. The 156 DC-2s that were built flew with airlines in the United States, Asia, and Europe. Thus in the colors of the Polish airline LOT, the Spanish carrier Iberia, Lufthansa, and, as already described, the Dutch airline KLM.

THE DC-3: AN AIRCRAFT FOR CYRUS ROWLETT SMITH

The next evolutionary step of the "DC" family was the result of a request by American Airlines president Cyrus Rowlett "C. R." Smith. He wanted to use an aircraft with fourteen double-decker beds on nightly transcontinental routes across the United States. They were to replace the airline's Curtiss Condor aircraft, which were already obsolete at the time and whose fuselage consisted of a tubular steel frame covered with fabric. To accommodate the beds, the DC-2's all-metal fuselage was widened, the cabin ceiling raised, the wingspan increased, and the tail redesigned. Initially called the Douglas Sleeper Transport (DST) in accordance with its original purpose, the DC-3 was born.

On December 17, 1935, the thirty-second anniversary of the Wright brothers' first powered flight, the Douglas Commercial Three took off on its maiden flight. And with it the model that was to finally make the aircraft works of Donald Wills Douglas world famous. Spurred on by the successful night flights by the TWA DC-2, C. R. Smith, president of the young American Airlines, approached Douglas with the request to develop a further improved type, which American planned to use on its own night flights across the United States. To lend weight to his request, Smith immediately ordered twenty aircraft of a type of which not even a single sketch existed. Douglas initially feared for the sales prospects of the DC-2, which was selling well, if a direct competitor were to emerge from its own ranks—but was then persuaded of the good prospects of a second development based on the DC-1. In keeping with the new type's planned employment, Douglas and American named the new addition to the fleet the Douglas Sleeper Transport. Twelve comfortable seats, each more than 3 feet wide, were installed in six individual compartments. Two of each formed a comfortable bed on night flights. In addition, a bunk bed could be folded down from the ceiling in each of these private areas. Directly behind the flight deck, there was also a "sky room" suite completely separated from the rest of the cabin, where two beds and a private bathroom provided individual luxury above the clouds.

After completing flight testing, Douglas delivered the first DST to American Airlines on June 7, 1936. Two months later, the DC-3, designed to carry twenty-one passengers on daytime flights, followed. United Air Lines, a Boeing subsidiary until 1934, took advantage of its new manufacturer-independent freedom and became the second DC-3 customer in November 1936. TWA, Braniff, Pan American, and the Dutch airline KLM followed with further orders for DST and DC-3 aircraft. By 1939, more than 90 percent of all domestic American passengers were traveling on the DC-3. The outbreak of World War II in September 1939—and at the latest, the US entry into the war in December 1941—led to a veritable boom in orders for the military variant, initially designated the C-47. Starting in 1942, Douglas delivered 965 C-47s and 2,954 C-47As to the US Army Air Force (USAAF) from its new plant in Long Beach, California. Another 2,300 C-47As and 3,064 C-47Bs were produced at Oklahoma City. The C-47 essentially differed from its civilian counterpart in having a large cargo door complete with structural reinforcements and a cabin that could be used for transporting troops or cargo, with no sound insulation. There were countless versions of the DC-3 in military use, including eight type designations alone for those aircraft acquired from various airlines. In addition to powered variants on wheels, floats, and skis, Douglas also developed an unpowered version as a cargo glider. The Douglas XCG-17 was intended to be towed by a C-47, but it never entered production.

Along with the USAAF, which called its aircraft Skytrain, and the US Navy's Skytrooper, the Royal Air Force was one of the largest operators of the C-47 series, which it christened the Dakota. RAF Dakotas earned a legendary reputation in 1948–49 as "candy bombers" during the Berlin Airlift, which delivered essential supplies to the people living in the western sectors of Berlin at the beginning of what remains to this day the largest humanitarian airlift. The DC-3 was also produced under license in Japan and the USSR. A total of 6,157 Lisunov Li-2s were produced in the Soviet Union. During World War II, Russia also received more than 700 US-made DC-3s equipped with Russian AS-62 engines and designated TS-62s.

After the end of the Second World War, the airlines demanded new aircraft that were faster and larger than the hundreds of DC-3/C-47s available from surplus military stocks. Spurred on by initially strong interest from the airlines, Douglas developed the Super DC-3. More-powerful engines, a longer fuselage for up to ten more passengers, a larger vertical stabilizer, and up to 50 percent greater range turned the original DC-3 design into a new and elegant airliner. But in the end, Douglas sold just three aircraft to Capital Airlines. Had the US Navy not had 100 of its own standard DC-3s, designated R4D-5 and -6, converted into R4D-8s, this program would have been a commercial flop. The latest DC-3 conversion still offered today is the Basler BT-67, developed by Basler Turbo Conversions. Based in Oshkosh, Wisconsin, the company replaces the DC-3's old Wright radial engines with modern Pratt & Whitney Canada PT6A-67R turboprops with Hartzell five-blade propellers. In addition, the cockpit instruments have been brought up to today's standards. After conversion, the DC-3s thus made fit for the twenty-first century not only are able to fly faster, higher, and farther than the standard version of 1935 but are also able to carry even more payload.

The list of aircraft types that have been marketed as "DC-3 replacements" is almost endless. The Fokker F-27 Friendship, the Handley Page Herald, the prototype Aviation Trader Accountant, and even the Bremer Jet VFW 614 all were doomed to failure, and, with very few exceptions, there is still no suitable replacement for the almost indestructible Dakotas. Even in 2022, DC-3s with their antiquated piston engines will continue to be used commercially in remote regions, but they will also be kept in airworthy condition around the globe by clubs and wealthy private individuals as a reminder of the pioneering days of air travel.

SIX BRITISH DAKOTAS

G-AIWD operated by BKS Air Transport of London. Photographed at Newcastle on November 3, 1962. *Tom Weihe*

G-AKJH of Gregory Air Services. Photographed at Newcastle on May 23, 1966. *Tom Weihe*

G-AMSS of Dan Air London. Photographed at Newcastle on September 19, 1966. *Tom Weihe*

SIX BRITISH DAKOTAS

G-AMYJ of South West Aviation. Photographed at Guernsey, Channel Islands, on September 23, 1969. *Tom Weihe*

G-AMYJ in service with Intra Jersey. Photographed at Jersey, Channel Islands, on September 15, 1973. *Tom Weihe*

G-AMYV of British Airways United. Photographed at Newcastle on May 20, 1966. *Tom Weihe*

CHAPTER 2
FROM DC-1 TO BASLER BT-67

The military hybrid combining the fuselage of the DC-2 with the wings, tail, and more-powerful engines of a DC-3 was designated the C-39 or C-42, depending on the type of engines fitted. *Douglas / Ron Handgraaf*

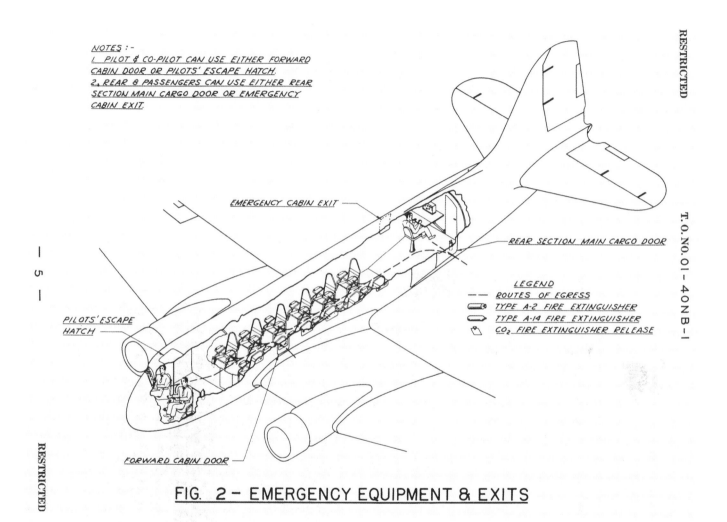

NOTES :-
1. PILOT & CO-PILOT CAN USE EITHER FORWARD CABIN DOOR OR PILOTS' ESCAPE HATCH.
2. REAR 8 PASSENGERS CAN USE EITHER REAR SECTION MAIN CARGO DOOR OR EMERGENCY CABIN EXIT.

EMERGENCY CABIN EXIT

REAR SECTION MAIN CARGO DOOR

LEGEND
ROUTES OF EGRESS
TYPE A-2 FIRE EXTINGUISHER
TYPE A-14 FIRE EXTINGUISHER
CO_2 FIRE EXTINGUISHER RELEASE

PILOTS' ESCAPE HATCH

FORWARD CABIN DOOR

FIG. 2 – EMERGENCY EQUIPMENT & EXITS

This drawing graphically illustrates the 1 + 1 seating arrangement of the narrow DC-2 fuselage employed by the C-39/C-42. *Douglas / Ron Handgraaf*

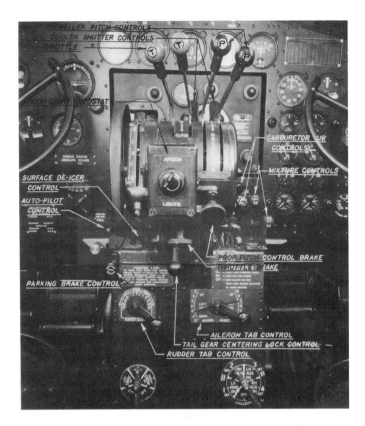
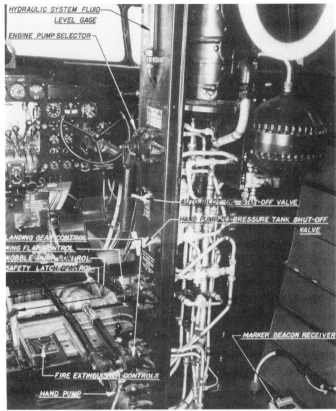

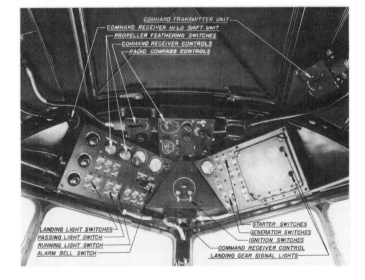

Detailed depiction of the cockpit of the C-39/C-42, a hybrid combining features of the DC-2 and DC-3. *Douglas / Ron Handgraaf*

A USAAF C-47 over the pyramids of Giza near the Egyptian capital of Cairo.
The reliable Skytrain also served in the North African theater during World
War II. *Photo courtesy of US Air Force*

The British Airspeed Ambassador (*taking off*) was one of many aircraft types that claimed to be a successor to the Dakota, an example of which is present in the foreground. *Author's archive*

BEA EUROPE'S FINEST AIR FLEET

The Viscount "Discovery" Class
(named after British Explorers)
40-47 passengers.
Four 1,550 h.p. Rolls-Royce Dart propeller turbines.
Span 94 ft.; cruising speed 328 m.p.h.

The "Elizabethan" Class
(named after famous Elizabethans)
47 passengers.
Two 2,500 h.p. Bristol Centaurus engines.
Span 115 ft.; cruising speed 250 m.p.h.

The "Pionair" Class
(named after pioneers of British Aviation)
32 passengers.
Two 1,200 h.p. Pratt and Whitney Twin Wasp engines.
Span 95 ft.; cruising speed 167 m.p.h.

The "Hebrides" Class
(named after medical pioneers)
17 passengers.
Four 250 h.p. de Havilland Gipsy Queen engines.
Span 71 ft. 6 in.; cruising speed 165 m.p.h.

The DC-3, which BEA designated the Pionair Class, is present in this historical British European Airways (BEA) brochure. *Author's collection*

G-ANLF was a C-47A Dakota operated by Air Kruise, a small British airline that was established in the county of Kent in 1946. In 1957, it was taken over by Silver City Airways, which in turn became part of British United Airways in 1962. In 1970, BUA was sold to the charter airline Caledonian, resulting in the creation of British Caledonian, which existed for many years. It was taken over by British Airways in December 1987 and merged with that airline in April of the following year. *Author's archive*

Two legends of aviation: the Junkers Ju 52/3m owned by the Deutsche Lufthansa Berlin Foundation, and the Lisunov Li-2 of a Hungarian association met at the Hamburg Airport Days in 2003. *Author's photo*

The NASA Flight Research Center's Douglas R4D-5/C-47H (Bu. No. 17136) in flight with its landing gear extended in 1963. The R4D was one of the workhorses for NACA and NASA at Edwards AFB from 1952 to 1984. Over those thirty-two years, three R4D aircraft served as utility transports, hauling personnel and equipment between NACA/NASA Centers and testing sites in and outside California. The R4D was used to tow the M2-F1, a lifting body built of mahogany plywood, into the air. The R4D towed the lifting body approximately 100 times, before the M2-F1 was retired for more-advanced lifting bodies dropped from a B-52 modified by NASA. *NASA*

A Douglas C-47 Skytrain known as "Whiskey 7" flying alongside a C-130J Super Hercules of the 37th Airlift Squadron over Germany, on May 30, 2014. The C-47 came to Ramstein for a week to participate in base activities with its legacy unit, the 37th Airlift Squadron, before returning to Normandy to re-create its World War II role and drop paratroopers over the original drop zone at Sainte-Mer Église in France. *US Air Force photo, taken by SSgt. Sara Keller / released*

Above: Members of the 37th Airlift Squadron gather for a group photo in front of the Douglas C-47 Skytrain designated "Whiskey 7" at Ramstein Air Base, Germany, on May 29, 2014. The 37th AS re-created the historical photo taken seventy years ago of the exact same aircraft with members of the 37th Troop Carrier Squadron. *US Air Force, photo by Airman 1st Class Jordan Castelan / released*

Below: Members of the same 37th Troop Carrier Squadron gather for a group photo in front and on Douglas C-47 "Whiskey 7" at RAF Cottesmore, England, in 1944. The photo on top of this page was recreated to honor their squadron's origin. *US Air Force*

Above and next two pages: "Puff the Magic Dragon" was the humorous nickname given to the first heavily armed AC-47 "Spooky" to see combat during the Vietnam War. The sequence of photos illustrates why this gunship richly deserved this nickname. All the General Electric M134 Miniguns mounted in the AC-47 fired from the port side of the fuselage from two window openings and the open cargo door. *Dr. John Provan*

AN OVERVIEW OF VERSIONS PRODUCED AND THEIR DESIGNATIONS

CIVIL DESIGNATIONS

Douglas DC-1	Prototype. Just one example built.
Douglas DC-2	First production version of the DC-1 with improved performance
Douglas Sleeper Transport	Initial version of the DC-3, originally built for night flights between the East and West Coasts of the United States. The type was developed at the behest of American Airlines, the launch customer.
Douglas DC-3	Standard day and night passenger version
BEA Express Freighter	Conversions of two British European Airways (BEA) DC-3s with two Rolls-Royce Dart turboprop engines. The two aircraft were used exclusively as freighters.
Pionair Class	DC-3 with the original piston engines operated by British European Airways (BEA)

World War II reenactors pose in front of a Douglas C-47 Skytrain at the D-Day 75th anniversary commemoration at the Air Mobility Command Museum, Dover Air Force Base, Delaware, May 4, 2019. *US Air Force photo by Mauricio Campino*

US ARMY AIR CORPS AND US ARMY AIR FORCE DESIGNATIONS

Douglas C-32	US Army Air Corps designation for the DC-2
Douglas C-33	Cargo version of the C-32
Douglas C-34	VIP version of the C-32. Just one example built.
Douglas C-38	Prototype of the C-39. Just one example built.
Douglas C-39	Hybrid of the fuselage of a DC-2 and the wings, empennage, and more-powerful engines of a DC-3
Douglas C-42	Like the C-39, but with more-powerful engines
Douglas C-47	Standard military transport version of the DC-3
Douglas C-47A	C-47 with 24-volt electrical system
Douglas C-47B	C-47 with superchargers and the provision for extra fuel tanks
Douglas C-47C	C-47 on floats
Douglas C-48	Civil DC-3s and DSTs requisitioned by the military after Pearl Harbor
Douglas C-49	DC-3s with Wright Cyclone engines impressed by the USAAF after the start of the war
Douglas C-50	Fourteen DC-3 airliners impressed off the production line by the USAAF, also powered by Wright Cyclone engines
Douglas C-51, C-52, C-68, and C-84	Civil DC-3s impressed by the USAAF, off the production or aircraft already in service
Douglas C-53	Dedicated troop transport developed from the DC-3 and used to carry US Army paratroopers
Douglas C-53A	Single example built with full-span slotted flaps and hot-air wing deicing
Douglas C-53B	Special version modified for cold weather and long range
Douglas C-53C	Like the C-53, but with a 24-volt electrical system
Douglas SC-47	Search-and-rescue version of the C-47
Douglas TC-47	Version of the C-47 for pilot training
Douglas RC-47	Reconnaissance version of the C-47
Douglas VC-47A and VC-47B	VIP versions of the C-47
Douglas XCG-17	C-47 converted into an assault glider
Douglas AC-47 "Spooky" Gunship	Heavily armed version of the C-47 employed during the Vietnam War
Douglas YC-129 and C-117	US Army Air Force designations for the Super DC-3
Skytrain	General designation for the C-47 in the American armed services
Skytrooper	Designation for the C-53 in the American armed services

THE DC-3 IN SERVICE WITH THE ROYAL AIR FORCE

Dakota I, II, III, and IV	Designations for C-47s in service with the British armed services, which received these aircraft from the United States as part of the Lend-Lease Agreement during World War II

US NAVY DESIGNATIONS

Douglas R4D-1	US Navy designation for the basic C-47
Douglas R4D-2	Designation for two Eastern Air Lines DC-3s impressed by the US Navy
Douglas R4D-3	Designation for the single C-53 acquired by the US Navy
Douglas R4D-4	Designation for ten DC-3s originally built for Pan American and used by the US Navy
Douglas R4D-5	US Navy designation for the C-47A
Douglas R4D-6 and R4D-7	US Navy designations for the C-47B
Douglas R4D-8X	Designation for the Super DC-3 prototypes acquired by the US Navy
Douglas R4D-8	Designation for 100 R4D-5s and D-6s converted to Super DC-3 standard by the US Navy

THE DC-3 IN THE SOVIET UNION

Lisunov Li-2	DC-3 built under license in the Soviet Union by the Lisunov Design Bureau
TS-62	700 DC-3s built in the United States and equipped with Russian AS-62 engines

CONROY AIRCRAFT CONVERSIONS

Conroy Turbo-Three	Two DC-3s equipped with Rolls-Royce Dart Mk. 510 turboprop engines from a crashed United Air Lines Vickers Viscount. The prototype was later converted into the Tri-Turbo Three.
Conroy Super Turbo-Three	Super DC-3 equipped with Rolls-Royce Dart turboprop engines. Production was limited to the prototype.
Conroy Tri-Turbo-Three	Conversion of an aircraft originally built as a C-53, with three Rolls-Royce Dart turboprop engines. In 1977, these were replaced by Pratt & Whitney of Canada PT-6A engines. The first flight by this unusual design, with one of its three engines mounted in the nose, took place on November 2, 1977. The aircraft was damaged by a fire in May 1986 but was rebuilt.

BASLER TURBO CONVERSIONS

Basler BT-67	Version with modern turboprop engines, lengthened fuselage, and glass cockpit, converted from original DC-3/C-47 aircraft by Basler in Oshkosh
C-47T Skytrain and AC-47T Gunship	Military versions of the BT-67

Above: This DC-3 with the registration D-CNSF was the only aircraft of the German airline Nordseeflug Lufttransport GmbH, founded in 1966. The photo was taken on May 17, 1967, at Hamburg Airport, Germany. *Courtesy of Tom Weihe*

Below: Founded in 1963 and existing until 1976, Rousseau Aviation was a French regional airline based at Dinard Airport in Brittany. In addition to DC-3s, it flew numerous Nord 262 turboprops as well as Hawker-Siddeley HS 748s on routes within France and to nearby countries. *Courtesy of Tom Weihe*

CHAPTER 3
BASLER BT-67
POLAR TRANSPORTS

The DC-3 was a beautiful, stable, and virtually indestructible airframe going to waste. We realized that by turbinizing and modernizing the airplane it would go on for many years. . . . For years the aviation industry had been searching for a replacement for this rugged and reliable aircraft . . . at Basler Turbo Conversions we're building it.
—Warren Basler (1926–1997)

As close to perfection as the piston-engined DC-3 was, Warren Basler believed there was a need for a better and more efficient version of this highly reliable aircraft. With that vision in mind, Basler Turbo Conversions was formed. Production began in January 1990 at the new 75,000-square-foot facility at Wittman Regional Airport in Oshkosh, Wisconsin. Since then, BT-67 aircraft have been manufactured and sold to customers around the world. In 1996, Jack Goodale, an aviation enthusiast and entrepreneur from Grand Rapids, Michigan, took over. Goodale brought his business background to the company and has continued to develop Basler in all areas. As a result, the BT-67 configuration of the DC-3/C-47 became a rare example of a successful historical aircraft fully adapted to the current market.

The two BT-67s of the German Alfred Wegener Polar Research Institute are operated on its behalf by the Canadian company Enterprise Air. Consequently, the aircraft have the Canadian civil registrations C-GAWI (Polar 5) and C-GHGF (Polar 6). *Johannes Käßbohrer, AWI*

Basler Turbo Conversions takes the legendary DC-3 and subjects it to a comprehensive overhaul process. Each airframe incorporates the know-how accumulated over the years, along with state-of-the-art components; reliable, quiet, and fuel-efficient Pratt & Whitney Canada PT6A-67R engines; and five-blade Hartzell propellers. The BT-67 modernization process includes a complete airframe overhaul, aerodynamic improvements, structural changes to increase strength and improve performance, and new systems to enhance reliability.

As the following listing shows, true to the legendary motto "The best replacement for a DC-3 is a DC-3," the BT-67 is in service with numerous customers around the globe. It is striking that the BT-67 often performs its duties under extreme climatic conditions, be it in high temperatures with high humidity over the jungles of South America and Asia, or—at the other extreme—in Arctic cold. Among the operators of BT-67 since October 1, 2007, is the German Alfred Wegener Institute (AWI). The state institution conducts research in the Arctic, Antarctic, and midlatitude and high-latitude oceans. It coordinates polar research in Germany and provides important infrastructure such as the research icebreaker *Polarstern* (Polar Star) and stations in the Arctic and Antarctic for international science. The Alfred Wegener Institute is one of the fifteen research centers of the Helmholtz Association, Germany's largest scientific organization.

FLIGHTS IN EXTREME CONDITIONS

It was not by chance that the AWI chose the Basler derivative of the DC-3. After all, the institute's two Basler BT-67 aircraft are specially equipped for flights in the extreme environmental conditions of the polar regions. The aircraft can take off and land on concrete, gravel, and snow runways with the help of a combined wheel-ski undercarriage. Deicing systems, heating mats for batteries and engines, and advanced navigation systems even allow instrument flight as well as landings in very difficult weather conditions and at freezing temperatures down to −54 degrees Celsius (−65° F). The aircraft's advantages over their Dornier Do 228-101 predecessors (Polar 2 and 4) are obvious: with a range of 2,900 kilometers (1,802 miles) and scientific equipment on board, Polar 5 and 6 can travel twice as far as the Dorniers. At the same time, the BT-67 has twice the payload and interior volume. The

The BT-67 is powered by modern Pratt & Whitney Canada PT6A-67R turboprop engines. *Uwe Nixdorf, AWI*

operating costs for the new birds are no higher than for Polar 2 and 4 combined. The BT-67s can take off and land at any point on the Greenland and Antarctic ice sheets; for example, at the German Kohnen station in Antarctica, which is some 3,000 meters (9,842 feet) above sea level, or at the Russian Vostok station, at an altitude of 3,477 meters (9,842 feet) above sea level.

The BT-67s were prepared for their first scientific mission in Antarctica in cooperation with the company Optimare Sensorsysteme in Bremerhaven, before the aircraft with Canadian civil registrations C-GAWI (Polar 5) and C-GHGF (Polar 6) were put into service. The aircraft had previously been operated by the Canadian company Enterprise Air Inc.

Scientists use the research aircraft to better understand processes in the polar regions and to record the interactions among the earth's crust, ice- and snow-covered areas, oceans, and atmosphere. Several times a year, Polar 5 and Polar 6 fly expeditions lasting several weeks in the Arctic and Antarctic. On board are various scientific instruments,

many of which were developed by the AWI itself. Depending on the purpose of the flight, additional—or different—equipment is installed. One example is the so-called EM Bird. Scientists use this torpedolike device to measure the thickness of sea ice in the polar regions—one of the most important parameters for measuring climate change. The EM Bird is suspended from a long cable below the aircraft to a level just 15 meters (49 feet) from the ground. The polar pilots carry out the measurement flights from Spitsbergen or the Canadian coast, for example, and fly out as far as 350 nautical miles during an EM Bird mission. The aircraft are also essential for logistics between the international research stations in Antarctica. The AWI participates in the international Dromlan network there. Within the framework of this logistics cooperation, Polar 5 and Polar 6 transport material and people between the various stations and are available to provide assistance in emergencies. Further research activities by these polar aircraft include geophysics, especially the mapping of the Antarctic continental plate, as well as determination of the geometry and dynamics of the adjacent continental plates. With the support of the aircraft, ice researchers, the so-called glaciologists, record the thickness of the ice and the internal structure of the Antarctic and Greenland ice sheets with the aid of radar surveys. Aircraft missions in atmospheric research and meteorology focus primarily on the study of minute particles in the air, known as aerosols.

Veteran DC-3 pilots would scarcely recognize BT-67's modernized cockpit.
Maike Thomsen, AWI

POLAR 5 AND POLAR 6 FACT SHEET

Name: Polar 5 (C-GAWI) || Polar 6 (C-GHGF)
Type: Basler BT-67
Manufacturer: Basler Turbo Conversions
Entered service with the Alfred Wegener Institute: 2007||2011
Length:20.66 meters (67.8 ft.)
Wingspan: 29 meters (95 ft.)
Empty weight: 8.3 metric tons (18,298 lbs.) (8.9 metric tons [19,621 lbs.] with ski undercarriage)
Power plants: Pratt & Whitney of Canada PT6A-67R turboprop engines
Engine output: 1,281 shaft horsepower
Fuel consumption: 570 liters (150.6 gallons) per hour
Maximum takeoff weight: 13 metric tons (28,660 lbs.)
Maximum takeoff elevation with no payload: 4,200 meters (13,779 ft.)
Range without payload: approx. 3,000 km (1,864 miles)
Range with 1,000 kg (2,204 lb.) payload: 2,300 km (1,429 miles)
Maximum cruise speed: 315 kph (195.7 mph) (indicated airspeed or IAS)
Minimum cruise speed: 167 kph (104 mph)
Crew: 2 pilots, 1 flight engineer
Scientists on board transport flight / measurement flight: 18/9

Note: Polar 5 and 6 are identical in many respects. In the overview, information about Polar 6 appears after this marking.

A BT-67 passes the German polar expedition ship Polarstern. *Alfred Wegener Institute / Thomas Krumpen* (CC-BY 4.0)

BASLER BT-67 OPERATORS

As the following overview of BT-67s active in the spring of 2022 shows, this type enjoys popularity with airlines, research facilities, and militaries around the world.

Bell Geospace
Base: Houston, Texas
Purpose: geophysical survey

Airborne Support
Base: Houma, Louisiana
Purpose: oil spill cleanup

Triangle Aviation
Base: Smithfield, North Carolina
Purpose: paratrooper training

Airtec
Base: California, Maryland
Purpose: polar operation, environmental research, survey

Mauritanian Air Force
Base: Nouakchott, Mauritania
Purpose: logistical support and ISR (reconnaissance)

Mali Air Force
Base: Bamako, Mali
Purpose: personnel and cargo transport

Spectrum Air Surveys
Base: Johannesburg, Republic of South Africa
Purpose: geophysical surveys

ALCI Aviation
Base: Oshawa, Ontario (Cape Town, Republic of South Africa)
Purpose: Antarctic operations, general transport, geophysical surveys

Kenn Borek Air
Base: Calgary, Alberta, Canada
Purpose: polar operations, environmental research

CGG
Base: Ottawa, Ontario, Canada
Purpose: geophysical survey

Cargo North
Base: Thunder Bay, Ontario, Canada
Purpose: high-frequency cargo

Colombian Air Force
Base: Bogotá, Colombia
Purpose: gunship for counterinsurgency operations

Colombian National Police
Base: Bogotá, Colombia
Purpose: logistical support for counternarcotic operations

El Salvadoran Air Force
Base: Ilopango, El Salvador
Purpose: troop and cargo transport

Guatemalan Air Force
Base: Guatemala City, Guatemala
Purpose: troop and cargo transport

Alfred-Wegener Institute
Operated by Enterprise Air, Canada
Base: Bremerhaven, Germany
Purpose: environmental research, polar logistics

Royal Thai Air Force
Base: Bangkok, Thailand
Purpose: water bombing, cloud seeding

Polar Research Institute of China
Base: Shanghai, China
Purpose: environmental research

Source: Basler Turbo Conversions

CHAPTER 4
THE HUMP

CHINA NATIONAL AVIATION CORPORATION

ABOVE THE ROOF OF THE WORLD

A subsidiary of American airline Pan American Airways (PAA), China National Aviation Corporation (CNAC) became a legend during World War II. It connected China, cut off by Japanese troops, with its Western allies, and the only way to do so was over the Himalayas—the tallest mountain range in the world.

In the 1930s, the German airline Lufthansa and the American PAA in particular were what today would be called "global players." From their respective home markets, they extended an airline network across continents and oceans. Once the intercontinental routes were established, they set up subsidiaries at the destination airports to handle onward transportation to distant continents. Examples include Brazil's Syndicato Condor Ltda. and Lufthansa's Chinese Eurasia, as well as PAA's CNAC, also based in the Middle Kingdom.

CNAC's twenty-year history began in 1929, when Curtiss-Wright, an American aircraft and aircraft engine manufacturer, decided to establish a Chinese mail airline. Called China Airways Federal (CAF), the airline was a subsidiary of North American Aviation Exploration Inc., itself part of the Curtiss Group. To obtain air rights in China, CAF cooperated with China National Airways, on whose behalf it carried airmail between Shanghai, Hankow, Nanking, and Beijing. But the Americans had bet on the wrong partner, because the Chinese Supreme Court ruled as late as 1929 that it was not Sun Fo, president of China National Airways and also China's postmaster general, who was responsible for airmail transport, but the Ministry of Communications. Its senior minister Wang Pei Chun also had ambitions to become active in the aviation business and founded Shanghai Chengtu Airways, which competed with CAF. The defeated Sun Fo had no choice but to vacate his post as president of China National Airways—and leave its management to his archrival Wang Pei Chun.

CNAC Douglas C-47 Skytrain photographed in flight. CNAC's distinctive "Chung" insignia was applied to aircraft in 1942 at the request of the 14th Air Force for identification purposes. The "Chung" character means "middle," and it refers to China being called the Middle Kingdom or Nation. *National Museum of the US Air Force / cnac.org*

CNAC Curtiss C-46 Commando cargo aircraft being unloaded in China. CNAC carried more than 10 percent of all cargo and personnel over the "Hump." *National Museum of the US Air Force / cnac.org.*

Occasionally—and probably mainly for PR photos—the US Army Air Force also used animals, in this case an elephant, to help load aircraft flying over the "Hump." *USAAF, Dr. John Provan*

After this Chinese internal intrigue, the Curtiss Group was initially faced with the shambles of its Chinese involvement. Only a new, unencumbered CAF management could now help. Max S. Polin and Minard Hamilton were sent from the United States to China as new airline directors. And they actually succeeded in convincing Minister Wang Pei Chun to cooperate. The result was the CNAC, a joint venture between Curtiss and the Chinese government. Under Chinese management, the new CNAC absorbed all the activities of China Airways Federal, China National Airways, and Shanghai Chengtu Airways.

On July 20, 1929, the *New York Times* reported that North American Aviation Exploration Inc. had given CNAC a one-million-dollar start-up loan. As collateral, Curtiss received a mortgage on CNAC's airfields and equipment, repayable within eight years.

The Western-oriented metropolis of Shanghai became the headquarters of the Chinese-American airline. It remained so even after PAA took over the 45 percent Curtiss share in April 1933. The Chinese continued to control the administration, while the Americans organized flight operations. It was not until the beginning of the Sino-Japanese War and the landing of Japanese troops on the Chinese Pacific coast that CNAC had to pull up stakes in Shanghai in 1937 and move to Hong Kong, which until then had been spared from hostilities. From 1941, the airline was connected to PAA's passenger service to San Francisco. A year earlier, the airline had already opened clipper routes from the American West Coast to Honolulu, Canton Island, and Noumea. The route to Singapore was added at the same time as Hong Kong. But all dreams of a dense Pan Am route network across the Pacific ended abruptly on December 7, 1941, with the Japanese navy's attack on the American Pacific base at Pearl Harbor. The horror of World War II had now reached the Pacific.

That same day, the Japanese air force attacked Wake Island, a Pacific atoll located halfway between Hawaii and the Philippines, and the PAA flying-boat station located there. The attack on the "Philippine Clipper" moored at the jetty and the base lasted just five minutes, but when it was over, the Pan Am Clipper station had been completely destroyed. Nine airline personnel were killed. Although machine gun fire had damaged the Martin 130 flying boat, the crew managed to get the "Philippine Clipper" back into shape. Time was pressing, because at any moment the survivors had to expect another attack by the Japanese. With all survivors on board, the completely overloaded flying boat made its third attempt to return to the United States. After three days and stops at Midway and Honolulu, the plane arrived at the port of San Francisco. Another Pan Am Clipper, also anchored in Hong Kong on December 7, 1941, was strafed by Japanese fighter planes and destroyed by fire. The crew and passengers of the "Pacific Clipper," on the other hand, experienced a true odyssey. The flying boat was en route from San Francisco to Auckland, New Zealand, when news of the Japanese attacks reached it. Rather than turn around and fly back to the United States across the Pacific Ocean, now controlled by enemy warships and fighter planes, the crew decided to continue the flight westward. Via New Zealand, Australia, India, the Middle East, and Africa, the flight path of the Pacific Clipper continued over the South Atlantic and the Caribbean toward the United States' East Coast. On the morning of January 6, 1942, the captain of the Pan Am flying boat checked in with the completely surprised air traffic controller at the seaplane station in New York Harbor with the words "Pacific Clipper, arriving from Auckland, New Zealand. Landing at Pan American Marine Terminal La Guardia in seven minutes." After one month and 31,500 miles, the Pan Am Clipper had involuntarily completed the longest flight distance ever flown by a civilian aircraft—and successfully completed its first trip around the globe.

THE HIMALAYAS: THE HUMP

One year before the occupation of Hong Kong by the Japanese on December 25, 1941, there were increasing signs that the war front along the Chinese coast was also going to reach the British Crown colony in the foreseeable future. Only three years after its escape from Shanghai, the CNAC management commissioned Charles L. Sharp and Hugh L. Woods to once again search for a safe location for the company headquarters. The new base had to be within easy reach of China, be close to a port or a railroad junction, and—above all—offer protection from Japanese attacks. The choice eventually fell on the port city of Calcutta in British-ruled India. Nevertheless, the CNAC fleet remained in Hong Kong until the last minute, participating in a spectacular seventy-two-hour airlift to evacuate 275 civilians from the surrounded city to Chungking, China.

With the Japanese armed forces in control of almost the entire Western Pacific and large parts of Southeast Asia by 1942, the Chinese government of Chiang Kai-shek was largely cut off from aid from Allied countries, most notably Great Britain and the United States. The situation seemed particularly precarious after the occupation of Burma (Myanmar) by Japanese units. They now formed an insurmountable barrier between India and the unoccupied parts of China. The only remaining supply route was the air corridor over the "roof of the world"—the Himalayas—with the 8,844-meter (29,015 foot) Mount Everest as its highest peak.

The China National Aviation Corporation crews took on this great challenge. Every flight was an adventure, as the lack of navigation aids and extreme weather with wind speeds of 160 kph (99.4 mph), icing, and dangerous downdrafts demanded all the pilots' skills. The fully loaded Douglas C-47s had to climb to altitudes of over 6,000 meters (19,685 feet)—and this with no oxygen supply for the pilots and passengers. If the crews flew over flatter terrain near the Burmese border, they faced the threat of Japanese air attacks. One CNAC airliner returned safely to its base with over 3,000 bullet holes. During the early years of the war, the airline flew under contract to the US Army Air Force's Flying Tiger Group, which became part of the USAAF as of July 4, 1942. From the occupation of Burma by Japanese troops in April 1942 until the end of the war in August 1945, CNAC aircraft transported some 114,500 tons of supplies over the Himalayas in the course of 38,000 flights.

At the end of hostilities, CNAC had one of the largest fleets within Asia, consisting of Douglas DC-3s and DC-4s and Curtiss C-46s. In the spring of 1946, CNAC returned its headquarters to Shanghai. However, the Chinese Civil War from 1947 to 1949 meant that CNAC was unable to continue its old successes. With the defeat of the military dictator Chiang Kai-shek by the Communists under Mao Zedong, the history of CNAC also came to an end. Shortly after 8:00 p.m. on December 31, 1949, its liquidation was sealed in room 231 of the Hong Kong and Shanghai Bank in the British Crown colony of Hong Kong.

Loading fuel drums into a Curtiss Commando for its next flight over the Himalayas. *USAAF, Dr. John Provan*

Nose art on "Sultan's Magic Carpet," a Douglas C-47 Skytrain assigned to Lt. Gen. Daniel Sultan, participating in the "Hump" operation. *USAAF, Dr. John Provan*

While the Curtiss C-46 bore the brunt of the "Hump" operation, it was feared by its crews because of its poor flight characteristics, especially on just one fully functioning engine. *USAAF, Dr. John Provan*

CHAPTER 5
"BEACH CITY BABY"

THE RESTORATION OF A DOUGLAS C-53-DO SKYTROOPER

The story of the Douglas C-53-DO Skytrooper with its new name "Beach City Baby" is exemplary of the countless Skytrains and Dakotas that served the Allied nations. At the airfield serving Beach City, a town of just under 1,000 people in Ohio, members of the nonprofit organization Vintage Wings Inc. helped restore this C-53 to airworthiness. It returned to the air in 2022 and has since found its final base at Franklin Venango Regional Airport in Pennsylvania.

With fewer than 400 examples completed, the C-53 Skytrooper accounted for a comparatively small share of the more than 10,000 Douglas DC-3 military models built. Compared to the C-47 Skytrain, the Skytrooper lacks its double cargo door on the aft port side of the fuselage, the reinforced cargo floor, and the more robust landing gear and wider propeller blades of its modified sister model. Notwithstanding this absence of additional military equipment present on a C-47, the C-53s also played a very important role during World War II. Among other things, they flew as troop transports, as drop planes for paratroopers, as glider tugs, and as air ambulances for the evacuation of wounded soldiers from combat zones. In addition to the large four-engine bombers, it was the tens of thousands of Douglas C-47s and C-53s that were responsible for the Allied success in World War II. This was confirmed after the end of hostilities by Gen. Dwight D. Eisenhower, who served the United States of America as its thirty-fourth president from 1953 to 1961. He cited the use of military DC-3 variants as one of the four most important factors in Allied victory in the global theaters of war.

Dubbed the Beach City Baby, the Vintage Wings Inc. C-53 was received factory-fresh by the US Army Air Corps on January 29, 1942, at Douglas in Santa Monica, California, and given the serial number 41-20095. It was first stationed at what was then Bolling Air Force Base in the US capital of Washington, DC, but shortly thereafter it was transferred to Presque Isle, Maine, where it was attached to the Air Corps Ferrying Command. Flown by pilots of Northeast Airlines who had been drafted into the war effort, "095" was one of the first aircraft to establish the airlift between the United States and Great Britain for troops and materiel during the war. As a result of the intensified fighting in North Africa, the C-53 was transferred there in November 1942 and flew troops and wounded to and from the battlefields on behalf of the North African Division of Air

Transport Command. The C-53 fulfilled its last military role as a drop plane for paratroopers in the conquest of Sicily before it was retired from service on May 12, 1945, at the Egyptian capital of Cairo.

But this was far from the end of the fascinating history of this aircraft, which from then on was used as a civilian DC-3. The Danish airline Det Danske Luftfartselskab (DDL) acquired the former C-53 from the American military and used it on its European route network. When it merged with the Norwegian DNL and the Swedish airlines ABA and SILA to form the Scandinavian Airlines System (SAS) on August 1, 1946, the Douglas—with the registration OY-DCE and the name "Gorm Viking"—also joined the integrated fleet of the new trinational airline. Northern Europe remained her home until 1952, when her path led back to the United States and the Rampo Foundry & Wheel Works in New York. After receipt by its new owner, the aircraft was given the civil registration N9959F. The Air Carriers Corporation was the next of many stations in the aircraft life of today's "Beach City Baby"—this time with the registration N34D.

But it wasn't until some twenty-one years after its delivery to the US Army Air Corps that the C-53 was to achieve a certain degree of notoriety—if only as the official transport aircraft of Ohio governor James Allen Rhodes. He was a great friend of aviation and made sure that airfields in Ohio mushroomed during his terms in office. His director of aviation affairs and DC-3 pilot Norm Crabtree is reported to have said, "The runway of an airport is the most important main street of a place." And true to that motto, numerous airports were rebuilt across the country, with Rhodes and Crabtree attending their opening ceremonies in their C-53, helping the aircraft achieve national prominence. Also called "Buckeye One" in reference to the horse chestnut (buckeye), the floral symbol of the state of Ohio, the plane flew for twenty years on behalf of the Republican governor Rhodes, whose terms lasted from 1963 to 1971 and from 1975 to 1983—as well as for Democratic governor John Joyce Gilligan in the interim. It also retired as a government machine in parallel with Rhodes's final departure from politics. The next stop for the aged Skytrooper was the United States Air Force Museum in Dayton, Ohio. It remained there when Athens-based Ohio University acquired the C-53 from the museum and registered it as N34DF. Their plan, however, was not to get this Douglas flying again, but to install its engines in a second DC-3 owned by the university to keep that aircraft airworthy. To this day, Ohio University uses simulators and its own fleet of aircraft to train students to become professional pilots and technicians, as well as aviation industry managers. The largest aircraft in the university fleet, which is stationed at the university's own airport, is currently a twin-engine Beechcraft Baron.

JASON CAPRA AND HIS "BABY"

So "Beach City Baby" remained at Dayton until Ken Joseph acquired the old-timer, bought functioning engines, and received permission from the US Federal Aviation Administration (FAA) for a one-time transfer flight to Beach City, Ohio. There, his involvement ended in 1992, and the C-53, with its long and varied history, was left to its fate and the wind and weather, sitting out in the open for many years. So it remained until, as in a fairy tale, in the summer of 2015, its prince in the form of Jason Capra drove past that airfield by pure chance and wakened the Skytrooper with a kiss. He couldn't believe his eyes when he spotted the silhouette of a DC-3. He immediately interrupted his journey toward home, and already during this first fateful encounter made the decision to save the aircraft. What followed was an extensive overhaul of the aircraft, which had been badly damaged over the years, which Capra and his enthusiastic team of volunteers embarked on in 2016. The legal framework for the project, which relies on donations, is the nonprofit Vintage Wings Inc. Although the Douglas never wore nose art during its military career, the restoration team christened it Beach City Baby as a reminder of its "discovery" by Jason Capra and the site of its restoration. Jason describes the naming process this way: "At the very beginning of the project, I always told my friends about 'my baby' in Beach

City when I told them about the C-53—so it was a logical step to one day christen her 'Beach City Baby.' We initially took the basic pinup design from historic World War II nose art photos. Ultimately, though, it was my fiancée, Emilee, whom Chad Hill of Django Studios, which specializes in nose art designs, among other things, used as the model for the artwork he designed and painted on the nose of the plane." Other nose art by Chad Hill adorns the nose sections both of the C-47s "That's All Brother" and "Do It" and the Consolidated B-24 "Ol' 927."

"BEACH CITY BABY": FIRST FLIGHT MAY 14, 2022

Pages 67–75: The Douglas C-53 "Beach City Baby" is one of the latest additions to the worldwide community of Douglas DC-3s operated by clubs and private individuals. *All photos on these pages by Jason Capra*

CHAPTER 6
DAKOTAS SAVE BERLIN

The Berlin Airlift of 1948 and 1949 was one of the largest, if not the largest, humanitarian aid operations ever carried out by air in human history. The background: Germany was divided in two after the end of the Second World War—into the western zones occupied by the United States, Great Britain, and France, on the one hand, and the Soviet Occupation Zone on the other. At first, there was no physical border separating the political blocks, but there was an insurmountable ideological wire mesh fence in the minds of the protagonists. In 1946, for example, the Soviets refused to hold talks with the Western Allies about a common future for the sectors of Germany they controlled. The situation escalated when, on June 18, 1948, the United States, France, and Great Britain jointly decided to impose currency reform in the zones of West Germany and the western sectors of Berlin under their control, which led to the introduction of the German deutsche mark. In response, the Soviets sealed off their occupation zone not only to West Germany but also to the western sectors of Berlin. From then on, there were no longer any road, rail, or water links to West Berlin. A forcible breakthrough and the creation of a land corridor to Berlin would inevitably have led to a military conflict with the Soviet Union. Thus, the only remaining supply routes were the three air corridors between the West German zones and the Allied sectors of West Berlin, which had been negotiated in 1945. These would have to provide the West Berliners, who were surrounded on all sides, with all the necessities of life.

In the weeks before the total blockade, which was to become a reality shortly thereafter, the Soviet Union provoked the Western Allies by obstructing their land and rail transports. The American military governor in Germany, Gen. Lucius D. Clay, therefore decided to organize a small airlift to supply US units stationed in Berlin, flying some 200 tons of material to Tempelhof from April 2 to 4, 1948.

On the night of June 23–24, 1948, things got serious for the 2.2 million West Berliners. From then on, barriers blocked all road, rail, and ship traffic into the Western Allied sectors, and West Berlin was cut off from its power supply in the Soviet Occupation Zone. In the search for the right response to the Soviet provocation, there was initially disagreement within the US administration.

president Truman. After Clay, anticipating what was to come, had ordered the establishment of an airlift to supply the Allied forces and the 2.2 million people living in Berlin's western sectors on June 25, President Truman confirmed his action three days later with the terse official statement "We are in Berlin and there we stay. Period."

On June 26, 1948, the first Douglas C-47s of the US Air Force and the British Royal Air Force took off for Berlin. While on the American side they were soon replaced by Douglas C-54M Skymasters, the aircraft christened the Dakota by the British, which served throughout the blockade. They were supplemented by Avro Tudor and York and Handley Page Hastings transports and Short Sunderland flying boats of the RAF. At the height of the airlift, which the British code-named "Operation Plainfare" and the US military referred to as "Operation Vittles," numerous civilian transport aircraft were also used, most of which were provided by smaller British airlines.

Time was of the essence, because on that fateful day in June 1948, West Berlin's supply depots held just enough food, gasoline, and coal to last two to three weeks. After that, the coal-fired power plants located in the western sectors would have gone out, and with them the electricity in the city. Trucks and cars would have come to a standstill, and people would have gone hungry from then on. The demand for food alone amounted to around 2,000 tons per day—compared with the capacity of a fully loaded Dakota of 2.5 tons. To make matters worse, the start of the airlift coincided with construction work on the only runway at Gatow Airport, which was in the British zone and was now being completed in a rush. Thus, Tempelhof in the US zone was the only landing site available at first. But the logistical and operational challenges did not end there. For example, the largest British airlift hub in West Germany, RAF Base Wunstorf, initially lacked everything. Even chocks to secure the fifty-four Dakotas and forty Avro Yorks stationed there from early July 1948 were in short supply. And then it started to rain! Not just a little, because soon the freighters at Wunstorf were sinking in the mud—and even the asphalt runway at Gatow often had to be closed briefly to clear the

The Dakota transports of the Royal Air Force and the DC-3s of numerous British airlines played a major role in the success of the Berlin Airlift in 1948–49. This photograph, showing the engine cover of the Dakota protruding from the cabin door, was taken in the summer of 1998 during a visit to Hamburg by the RAF Battle of Britain Memorial Flight's Dakota. *Author's photo*

Withdrawal from Berlin was considered, as was military liberation of the city by means of an attack across the Soviet Occupation Zone. A central role was played by Gen. Clay, who vehemently advocated that the Western Allies remain in Berlin and whose unbending attitude impressed US

"Camel Caravan to Berlin" was probably the most famous Skytrain flown by the US Air Force. It carried the camel "Clarence" along with 5,000 pounds of candy to Berlin on October 21, 1948. The little camel was the mascot of the American 86th Fighter Squadron, stationed at Neubiberg, Bavaria. During the unit's previous assignment in Libya, 1Lt. Don Butterfield had been offered the camel for $50—and he bought it. When the Berlin blockade began, the unit's personnel decided that the children of the besieged city needed that very camel to cheer them up. So it was flown to Berlin as "air cargo" on that very C-47. *US Air Force*

water from the runway. Even worse, the incessant rain caused the C-47s' cables and electrical boxes to get wet, and unserviceability levels rose. On July 2, RAF had to temporarily ground twenty-six of its Douglas transports stationed at Wunstorf alone for this reason. In addition to the lack of operational aircraft, there was also an acute shortage of personnel—and a lack of suitable accommodation for the support personnel on the ground as well as for the flight crews. As a result, many crew members had to sleep in soaked tents, right next to the aircraft, amid the roar of their engines and the trucks delivering supplies. And yet, it was a minor miracle that the Royal Air Force was able to reach its target of 840 tons a day arriving in Berlin by air as early as July 14. The larger Avro Yorks, with a load capacity of 7.5 to 8.25 tons, but also the increase in the Dakota payload by about 25 percent to 3.3 tons contributed to this. The latter was achieved by dispensing with safety equipment and reducing the amount of fuel carried in the C-47s' wing tanks. The military Dakotas were flown primarily by British crews, but also by aircrews from the Commonwealth countries of Australia, New Zealand, and South Africa.

In the late 1940s, large flying boats were still very popular not only with British airlines but also with the Royal Air Force. Two squadrons flew the Short Sunderland between Hamburg and Berlin starting on July 4, 1948. The aircraft's saltwater-resistant hull was ideal for carrying food salt for the population of the enclosed city. But meat, sanitary napkins, and cigarettes were also regular cargoes bound for Berlin, where the majestic flying boats touched down on Lake Havel to cheers from the population. On the way back, the Sunderlands flew industrial goods manufactured in West Berlin during the blockade, such as lightbulbs from the Siemens factories, and passengers to the west. The operation was based at the then Blohm & Voss aircraft works in Hamburg-Finkenwerder, located on the Elbe River—today's Airbus plant, where A320-series aircraft currently undergo final assembly.

There was initially a dispute between the Americans and the British as to whether both cargo and people should be flown out of Berlin. The very tightly timed flight schedule of the US Air Force in particular did not permit any delays or longer loading times at Berlin-Tempelhof. So the Royal Air Force took over this task and, in the course of the airlift, flew a total of 35,843 tons of goods and mail as well as 131,436 passengers—mainly citizens of Berlin, including numerous children, the sick, and the elderly, but also refugees, including the author's grandparents and mother—out of the Soviet Occupation Zone and to the West.

In addition to food, the airlift's focus was on supplying Berlin with fuels, especially for vehicles, power plants, industry, and home heating. In addition to the coal shipments, which were flown mainly by the Douglas C-54 Skymasters of the US Air Force, the Royal Air Force exclusively organized the supply of the city with liquid fuels. Since only a few of the RAF's Avro 691 Lancastrians were

Parked on the ramp of the US Air Force base at Wiesbaden, C-47s wait for
their next mission. *US Air Force*

available, the British Foreign Office hired a whole fleet of civilian tankers. Thus, aircraft of this type operated by British South American Airways, Skyways, and Flight Refueling delivered fuel to the Berlin population. Their fuselages were retrofitted with a tank developed by British aviation pioneer Sir Alan Cobham. Cobham, who had founded the company Flight Refuelling Ltd. and developed the technique of air-to-air refueling, thus contributing significantly to the success of "Operation Plainfare."

But it was not only the civilian operators of the Avro Lancastrian who flew relief supplies to Berlin on behalf of the British Foreign Office. The Douglas C-47 was used by Air Contractors, Air Transport, British Nederland Air Services, Ciro's Aviation, Hornton Airways, Kearsley Airways, Scottish Airlines, Sivewright Airways, Trent Valley Aviation, and Westminster Airways. Without exception, these were small airlines that had few aircraft and even less experience. The airlines, which were paid on the basis of their actual "flying time" and the type of aircraft used, transported about 750 tons to Berlin per day. The fact that their civilian radios were initially unable to communicate with the military units, and that it took a major search in Great Britain to find the appropriate radio crystals, which were very rare at the time, to change the frequencies of the analog equipment, was only one of many remarkable facets of this operation. Most of the airlines contracted to take part in the airlift went bankrupt at the end of their contracts in August 1949, having been unable to find follow-up employment.

The multitude of military and civilian types, and the different cruising speeds of those aircraft, posed a special challenge to the organizers of the airlift. In order to guide this jumble of types through the three corridors in a coordinated and safe manner, the US and British air forces created a joint USAF/RAF headquarters called the Combined Airlift Task Force (CALTF). Maj. Gen. William H. Tunner devised the so-called block system for this purpose. Each airlift station in West Germany was assigned a time window within which aircraft had to be at the end of the air corridor to Berlin. Aircraft assigned to a block had a full thirty seconds to get there, which the Royal Air Force planes did

particularly well. Unlike the American transports, they were equipped with radar and distance-measuring equipment (DME) based on the radio beacon at Frohnau near Gatow, and kept the aircraft flying the northern corridor on course. Also, unlike on the US Air Force's C-47s and C-54s, the British carried a navigator. The American pilots, on the other hand, had to rely on their radio compasses and calculate ground speeds themselves, relying on the predicted wind strengths and directions. This meant that they were not always 100 percent correct.

There was a safety buffer of six minutes between the last aircraft of one block and the first of the following block. Each British airlift base was assigned its own flight altitude band, which on the route from Lübeck to Gatow, for example, was between 5,000 and 5,500 feet. Each of the various types had its own altitude for the flights to and from Berlin, so that no collisions could occur. The final approach to Berlin was then controlled by GCA (ground-controlled approach radar) or, if visibility was good, by the tower controllers.

It is amazing that the British civil aircraft taking part in the airlift were involved in just five fatal accidents in which the crews lost their lives in the service of West Berliners. How challenging it was to fly on the airlift was shown by September 1948, when Soviet air defenses began to hold exercises in the air corridors and repeatedly came dangerously close to the transports with their fighter jets. In all, the RAF made use of twenty-two airlines, operating ten different aircraft types and carrying 54,635 tons of cargo and 92,282 tons of liquid fuels to Berlin over the course of the blockade.

British airlines' participation in "Operation Plainfare" was coordinated through British European Airways (BEA) as the liaison organization in West Germany. BEA merged with BOAC in 1974 to form today's British Airways.

On May 12, 1949, the Soviet blockade came to an end, nine days after a "Four Power Communiqué" announcing an end to the blockade and counterblockade had been agreed to by representatives of the governments of the United States, Great Britain, France, and the Soviet Union. Nevertheless, the airlift could not be stopped from one day to the next,

Left: With its Dakota, the Royal Air Force honors not only the Battle of Britain, but also its participation in the Berlin Airlift. *Royal Air Force*

Below: Before the airlift could reach its full scope, a number of West German airfields, including Celle, had to be massively expanded to accommodate large numbers of aircraft and personnel. *Royal Air Force*

since first the city's food and fuel stores had to be replenished, and it continued until September of that year. The last official flight under the British Operation Plainfare took place on September 6, while the US Air Force ceremoniously ended its "Operation Vittles" on September 30, 1949.

AIRLIFT AIRFIELDS IN THE BRITISH ZONE

Schleswigland
Lübeck
Hamburg-Fuhlsbüttel
Hamburg-Finkenwerder
Fassberg
Celle
Wunstorf

AIRLIFT AIRFIELDS IN THE AMERICAN ZONE

Wiesbaden
Frankfurt Rhein/Main

AIRLIFT AIRFIELDS IN THE ALLIED ZONE IN WEST BERLIN

Tempelhof (American zone)
Gatow (British zone)
Tegel (French zone)

THE FOLLOWING AIRCRAFT WERE ALSO USED IN THE BERLIN AIRLIFT

Avro 685 York
Manufacturer: A. V. Roe & Company Ltd., Great Britain
Wingspan: 102 ft.
Length: 78.4 ft.
Height: 16.7 ft.
Power plants: 4 Rolls-Royce Merlin 502s
Cruise: approx. 217 mph
Range: approx. 1,243 miles
Up to forty Avro 685 York aircraft operated by the airlines Airflight, Skyways, and BSAA and the Royal Air Force took part in the Berlin Airlift in 1948–49. This type, which could carry up to 10.5 tons of freight, was the backbone of British operation, delivering 61 percent of the freight flown to Berlin by the British and accounting for 42 percent of flight movements. The aircraft used the northern sector of the air corridor leading to Berlin and returned to their six north German bases via the central corridor.

The Avro York was based on the design of the Avro Lancaster bomber, from which it took the wings, landing gear, Rolls-Royce Merlin engines, and tail unit. These assemblies were supplemented by a new, box-shaped fuselage on which a third fin and rudder provided improved maneuverability. The type entered service with the Royal Air Force as a troop carrier and freighter in 1942, but the York found new civilian use with British Overseas Airways Corporation (BOAC) and British South American Airways (BSAA), as well as Argentina's Flota Aérea Mercante Argentina (FAMA) after the war ended. In addition, the York flew with just about every postwar British private charter airline. The last two of 253 Avro 685s built are on display at the British Air Force Museum in Cosford and the Imperial War Museum in Duxford.

Avro 691 Lancastrian
Manufacturer: A. V. Roe & Company Ltd., Great Britain
Wingspan: 102 ft.
Length: 77 ft.
Height: 19.35 ft.
Power plants: 4 Rolls-Royce Merlin XXIVs
Cruise: approx. 248 mph
Range: approx. 4,101 miles
In 1942, Canada's Victory Aircraft Ltd. began converting a license-produced A. V. Roe (Avro) Lancaster bomber into a transport aircraft. The Toronto-based company replaced the nose glazing with a streamlined fairing, removed the dorsal gun turret, and installed an aerodynamically shaped tail cone in place of the tail turret. New cabin windows completed the conversion package for the aircraft, which was given the registration CF-CMS. From March 1943 onward, it was based at Dorval, near Montreal. The Canadian concept of a "swords to plowshares" conversion of the

RAF Control Gatow guided the numerous types of aircraft taking part in the British Operation Plainfare. *Royal Air Force*

Lancaster bomber also convinced the British company A. V. Roe, the developer and original producer of this type, and it in turn converted a number of bombers into civil aircraft for the BOAC. These twenty examples of the Avro 691 Lancastrian were used mainly for Asian destinations of the British long-haul airline.

Avro 688 Tudor
Manufacturer: A. V. Roe & Company Ltd., Great Britain
Wingspan: 120 ft.
Length: 105 ft.
Height: 24.25 ft.
Power plants: 4 Rolls-Royce Merlin 621s
Cruise: approx. 236 mph
Range: approx. 2,361 miles
After the end of the Second World War, the British state airline BOAC had to make do with a mix of flying boats and land-based aircraft, all of which were converted military aircraft that were ill suited for passenger service. In keeping with the British government's "Buy British" doctrine, BOAC management therefore hoped for the rapid development of modern domestically produced commercial aircraft. One of these hopefuls was the Avro Tudor, the prototype of which took off on its maiden flight on June 14, 1945. The Tudor proved to be an excellent freighter during the Berlin Airlift. BSAA participated in supplying the western zones of Berlin with seven aircraft, while Airflight operated two.

Bristol 170 Freighter
Manufacturer: Bristol Aeroplane Company, Filton, Great Britain
Wingspan: 108 ft.
Length: 68 ft.
Height: 21.5 ft.
Power plants: 2 Bristol Hercules 734s
Cruise: approx. 186 mph
Range: approx. 808 miles
Although originally planned as a military transport, the Bristol 170 achieved fame as a flying Channel ferry. Silver City Airways was the first airline to fly a Bristol 170 from Lympne in Great Britain to Le Touquet in France, on July 14, 1948. During the Berlin Airlift, two Bristol 170s were used by the British charter airline Airwork to fly bulky equipment to Berlin.

Handley Page H.P. 67 Hastings
Manufacturer: Handley Page, Radlett, Great Britain
Wingspan: 113 ft.
Length: 81.7 ft.
Height: 22.6 ft.
Power plants: 4 Bristol Hercules 101s
Cruise: approx. 310 mph
Range: approx. 3,106 miles
Equipped with tailwheel landing gear, the Handley Page H.P. 67 Hastings was developed as a troop carrier and freighter for the British air force. Up to twenty-four examples were stationed at Schleswigland (Jagel) from November 1948 for the duration of the airlift, carrying up to 10 tons of coal to the occupied city on each operational flight. Four of the 151 Hastings built are still preserved in museums around the world—and one of them can be seen in front of Berlin's Allied Museum. It arrived there on September 21, 1997, hanging on a hook under a large Mil Mi-26T helicopter of the Russian Federation, coming from Gatow Airport. What a conciliatory signal this was between the former adversaries in the blockade of West Berlin in 1948–49.

Handley Page H.P. 70 Halton
Manufacturer: Handley Page, Radlett, Great Britain
Wingspan: 104 ft.
Length: 70 ft.
Height: 20.7 ft.
Power plants: 4 Bristol Hercules'
Cruise: approx. 248 mph
Range: approx. 1,243 miles
The Handley Page Halton was a "swords to plowshares" conversion of former Halifax bombers into commercial aircraft on behalf of BOAC. Twelve of them flew from 1946 on various scheduled services from London to Africa and

Loading freight into a C-47 of the USAF's European Air Transport Service. *US Air Force*

India. BOAC used its H.P. 70s until 1948, selling them to private British airlines in the same year. The twelve Haltons and other Halifaxes converted into civil aircraft were also used in the Berlin Airlift. In a total of 8,162 flights, the forty-one aircraft operated by British American Air Services, Bond Air Services, Eagle Aviation, Lancashire Aircraft Corporation, Skyflight, World Air Freight, and Westminster Airways carried an impressive 31,082 tons of coal and 21,728 tons of fuel from airfields in northern Germany to West Berlin.

Short S.45 Solent / S.25 Sunderland
Manufacturer: Short Brothers, Rochester, Great Britain
Wingspan: 112.5 ft.
Length: 87.6 ft.
Height: 34.3 ft.
Power plants: 4 Bristol Hercules 637s
Cruise: approx. 242 mph
Range: approx. 1,802 miles
Both the Royal Air Force and the long-haul airline BOAC continued to operate a number of flying boats after the end of World War II. These included the Short Solent, which in BOAC parlance were referred to as Hythe Class machines. In May 1948, Aquila Airways acquired most of the former BOAC flying boats and used them, among other things, on the Berlin Airlift between Hamburg-Finkenwerder and Havelsee in West Berlin. In addition to these civil flights, Short Sunderland flying boats of Royal Air Force Coastal Command also carried freight to Berlin, mainly the 38 tons of salt needed daily. Their service ended only after Lake Havel froze over in early December 1948 and water landings were no longer possible.

Vickers VC.1 Viking
Manufacturer: Vickers-Armstrongs Ltd., Weybridge, Great Britain
Wingspan: 89.2 ft.
Length: 65 ft.
Height: 24 ft.
Power plants: 2 Bristol Hercules 634s
Cruise: approx. 261 mph
Range: approx. 1,118 miles
Developed from the Wellington bomber, the Vickers VC.1 was the first new type brought to market by the British aviation industry after the end of the war. Its maiden flight took place on June 22, 1945, and production ended three years later after even a jet-powered variant had left the factory. The British airline Transworld Charter operated two Vickers VC.1s on supply flights to Berlin during the airlift.

AIRLIFT QUOTES
Gen. Sir Brian Robertson (British military governor in Germany in April 1948): "As long as the majority of the Berlin population continues to oppose the Communists, the Russians will achieve nothing."

Robertson again, in a telephone conversation with RAF headquarters in Germany on June 24, 1948: "Something has to happen, and it has to happen immediately."

Telephone conversation between General Lucius D. Clay, American military governor in Germany, and Lt. Gen. Curtiss E. LeMay, US Air Force commander in Europe, on June 24, 1948:

> Clay: "Do you have aircraft that can transport coal?"
> LeMay: "Transport what?"
> Clay: "Coal."
> LeMay: "I don't understand. It sounds like you are asking me for aircraft that can transport coal."
> Clay: "That's exactly what I mean."
> LeMay: "The air force can transport anything."

THE BERLIN AIRLIFT IN NUMBERS
Amount of food delivered: 538,025 tons
Amount of coal delivered: 1,586,556 tons
Amount of fuel, military supplies, and other goods delivered: 201,266 tons
Number of flights: 555,370
Air miles flown: 104,358,951
Passengers flown to and from Berlin: 228,454

This indicator was used by the Royal Air Force to keep track of the target number of sorties for the day and the number actually flown. *Royal Air Force*

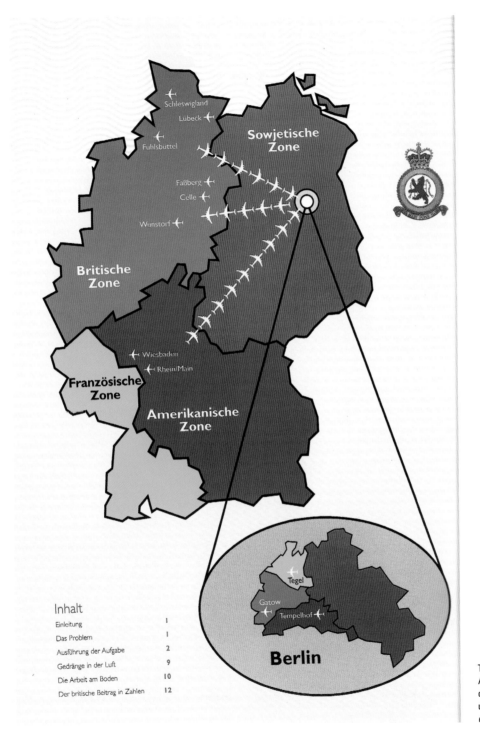

Schleswigland

Lübeck

Fuhlsbüttel

Sowjetische Zone

Faßberg

Celle

Wunstorf

Britische Zone

Wiesbaden

Rhein/Main

Französische Zone

Amerikanische Zone

Tegel

Gatow

Tempelhof

Berlin

This diagram shows the location of the Allied airfields in the western zones of occupation and the three air corridors used to supply Berlin from the air. *British embassy in Germany*

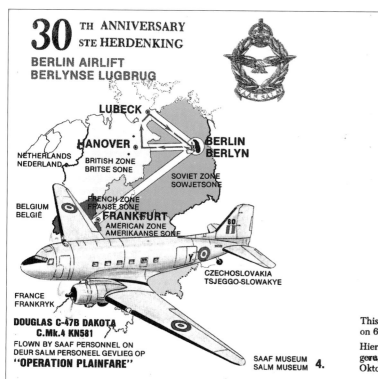

30TH ANNIVERSARY
STE HERDENKING

BERLIN AIRLIFT
BERLYNSE LUGBRUG

LUBECK

HANOVER

NETHERLANDS
NEDERLAND

BRITISH ZONE
BRITSE SONE

BERLIN
BERLYN

SOVIET ZONE
SOWJETSONE

BELGIUM
BELGIË

FRENCH ZONE
FRANSE SONE

FRANKFURT

AMERICAN ZONE
AMERIKAANSE SONE

CZECHOSLOVAKIA
TSJEGGO-SLOWAKYE

FRANCE
FRANKRYK

**DOUGLAS C-47B DAKOTA
C.Mk.4 KN581**

FLOWN BY SAAF PERSONNEL ON
DEUR SALM PERSONEEL GEVLIEG OP
"OPERATION PLAINFARE"

SAAF MUSEUM
SALM MUSEUM   **4.**

This cover was flown in Douglas C-47B Dakota Mk IV, 6857, of No 44 Squadron on 6 October 1979 from AFB Swartkop to Sishen, near the Army Combat School.

Hierdie koevert is per lug vervoer vanaf LMB Swartkop na Sishen, naby die Leërgeregskool, in 'n Douglas C-47B MK IV Dakota No 6857 van 44 Eskader, op 6 Oktober 1979.

Above: British Dakotas were also flown by crews from various Commonwealth countries during the airlift. South African participation is commemorated by this envelope, which flew in a South African Air Force C-47, in 1979. *Author's collection*

Below: Civil airlines, like Lancashire Aircraft Corporation, played a vital role for the success of the British participation at the Berlin Air Lift. Pictured is a Handley Page Halifax C.Mk. VIII. This particular aircraft was damaged beyond repair July 6, 1949, when the undercarriage collapsed upon landing at RAF Schleswigland on an airlift sortie. Luckily none of the three occupants were injured. *Royal Air Force*

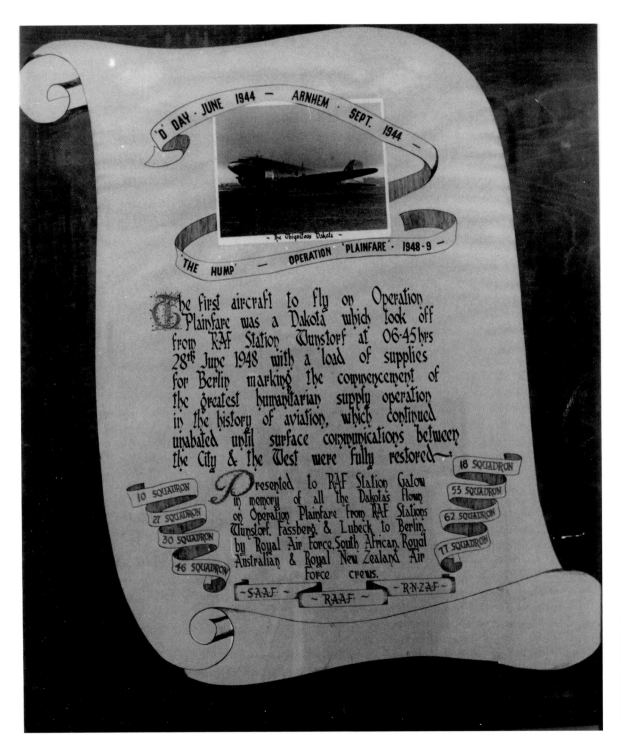

This sign, commemorating the start of "Operation Plainfare," was bequeathed to the RAF station at Berlin-Gatow. *Royal Air Force*

Based at the British Channel airfield of Ferryfield, Bristol 170 Freighters of Silver City Airways also took part in the Berlin Airlift. *Author's collection*

Loading cargo into a DC-3 of British European Airways. BEA coordinated operations by the various airlines that took part in the Berlin Airlift. *Author's collection*

A ramp full of Dakotas at Fassberg Airport, located in the British zone.
Royal Air Force

A Royal Air Force crew inspect their Dakota prior to takeoff. *Royal Air Force*

British military aircraft also carried passengers from Berlin-Gatow to the western zones. Among them were numerous children and refugees who had fled the Soviet Occupation Zone (SBZ) to the western sectors of Berlin. Among them were the author's mother and grandparents. *Royal Air Force*

Above: The Avro Lancastrian was particularly useful for transporting fuel to Berlin. *Royal Air Force*

A British Handley Page Halifax C.Mk. VIII (front) and two H.P. 70 Halton are serviced at Hamburg Airport. The West German Hanseatic City was a cornerstone of the British supply flights to Russian occupied West-Berlin. *Dr. John Provan*

The Avro York transports of the Royal Air Force and various British airlines were also able to carry large quantities of cargo. *Royal Air Force*

Hamburg Airport was another British airlift base. Here, two Handley Page Halton/Halifax transports of Bond Air Service wait for their next flight to Berlin. *Author's collection*

A Short Sunderland of the RAF docked on a lake in West Berlin. *Royal Air Force*

A packed airlift airfield with Bristol 170 Freighters of Silver City Airways and Avro Yorks of the Royal Air Force. *Royal Air Force*

The Avro Tudor was not a success as a passenger aircraft, and a number of them were lost in crashes, which helped create the legend of the so-called Bermuda Triangle. However, the type proved its worth as a cargo carrier during the Berlin Airlift. *Royal Air Force*

The Airlift Memorial at Frankfurt Airport commemorates the largest airborne humanitarian relief effort to date. *Dr. John Provan*

Two iconic noses. In the foreground is the C-47 of the Frankfurt Airlift Memorial, and behind it a Lockheed C-5 Galaxy of the US Air Force. *Dr. John Provan*

The difference in size between the Douglas C-47 Skytrain and the Lockheed C-5 Galaxy illustrates the great strides made in aircraft design. The diagram also speaks volumes about the small number of flights that would have been required if an aircraft the size of a C-5 had been available during the Berlin Airlift. *Dr. John Provan*

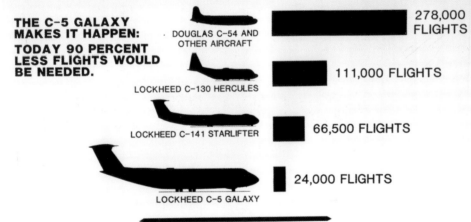

THE C-5 GALAXY MAKES IT HAPPEN: TODAY 90 PERCENT LESS FLIGHTS WOULD BE NEEDED.

DOUGLAS C-54 AND OTHER AIRCRAFT — 278,000 FLIGHTS

LOCKHEED C-130 HERCULES — 111,000 FLIGHTS

LOCKHEED C-141 STARLIFTER — 66,500 FLIGHTS

LOCKHEED C-5 GALAXY — 24,000 FLIGHTS

ABOUT 278,000 FLIGHTS WERE USED TO HAUL 2.34 MILLION TONS TO BERLIN DURING THE BERLIN AIRLIFT. A VARIETY OF AIRCRAFT WERE USED DURING THE AIRLIFT INCLUDING C-47 SKYTRAINS AND C-54 SKYMASTERS. TODAY, WITH LARGER TRANSPORT AIRCRAFT, LESS FLIGHTS WOULD BE NEEDED TO COMPLETE THE AIRLIFT. IN MANY WAYS, THE BERLIN AIRLIFT USHERED IN THE PRESENT ERA OF BIG AIRCRAFT USED BY THE MILITARY AIRLIFT COMMAND TODAY - - AIRLIFTERS WHICH ALSO HAVE HELPED SAVE PEOPLE AND NATIONS IN OTHER MORE RECENT TIMES OF NEED.

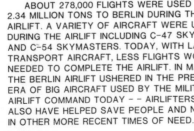

CHAPTER 7
IN PASSENGER SERVICE

SCANDINAVIAN DAKOTAS IN GERMANY

Until the new Lufthansa began operating on April 1, 1955, SAS filled the role of West German "national carrier." Its dense network of routes inside Germany and the European and intercontinental routes it offered from Germany literally gave wings to the German economic miracle of the 1950s. The first airline to return to war-ravaged Germany after 1945 was the Danish carrier Det Danske Luftfartselskab. Founded in 1918, and thus the oldest remaining airline in the world, now the Danish partner in SAS, it launched its first air service linking Copenhagen with Warnemünde and Hamburg in 1920. Building on this tradition, DDL's first Douglas DC-3 landed at Frankfurt's Rhein-Main Airport, then administered by the US Air Force and still showing evidence of the destruction caused by the war, on August 14, 1946. The only passenger who disembarked was the Dane Poul Heiberg Christensen. In the first DDL regional director's baggage were several bottles of fine Danish aquavit! The first bottle was opened during negotiations between Christensen and Col. Daniels, the American commander of the airfield, and ensured a smooth start for the airline's maiden flight between Copenhagen, Frankfurt/

Loading cargo into a SAS DC-3 at Stuttgart Airport. The capital of the state of Baden-Württemberg was then, and is now, the home to major companies such as Daimler-Benz, Porsche, and Bosch—and thus an important destination for air freight. *Stuttgart Airport*

Main, and Zurich, planned for the following day. Incidentally, Christensen was not only the first DDL representative in Germany, but the first airline representative in postwar Germany period!

The Swedish carrier ABA and the Norwegian operator DNL maintained routes in their own countries, until, in 1948, the three airlines established a dense network of routes inside Germany under the SAS banner. With the approval of the Western occupying powers, Scandinavian Airlines System assumed the role of the West German "national carrier" until the new Lufthansa began operations on April 1, 1955. With Frankfurt/Main as its hub, SAS propeller-driven airliners linked the cities of Hamburg, Hanover, Bremen, Düsseldorf, Stuttgart, Nuremberg, and Munich. The airline first operated Douglas DC-3s, followed by the more luxurious Convair CV-440 Metropolitan. The latter type's spacious seating layout made it very popular with passengers. SAS also operated the Douglas DC-6 and DC-6B, four-engined, long-range airliners, on its domestic German route network. Then, in the winter of 1959–60, Scandinavian became the first airline to offer jet service on its German routes with the SE 210 Caravelle.

In 1950, SAS offered sixteen routes within the Federal Republic, more than any other airline. This compared to nine offered by British European Airways (BEA) and six by the American airline Pan Am. A typical passenger spent three hours and forty-five minutes on a Scandinavian DC-3 flying route SK 614 from Frankfurt/Main to Hamburg, with stops at Düsseldorf and Bremen. The airline's 1954–55 winter schedule, its last before Lufthansa commenced operations, comprised ninety-six domestic German flights, making SAS the undisputed market leader among airlines.

After the West German currency reform of 1948, SAS literally gave wings to the tentative beginnings of the economic miracle, with a drastic expansion of its services. In addition to the domestic German routes, the Scandinavians operated almost their entire intercontinental route network and flights to the major European cities via West German airports at the beginning of the 1950s.

In the 1950s, tickets for a domestic SAS DC-3 flight were packaged in ticket sleeves such as this one. *Author's collection*

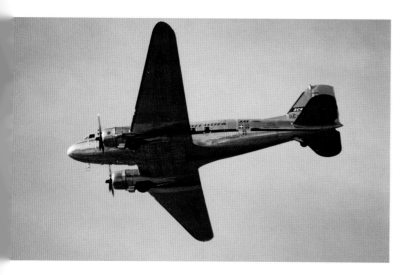

The DC-3 of the Swedish Flying Veterans Association is painted in the exact same livery as that used by SAS Dakotas used for scheduled flights to West Germany. *Author's photo*

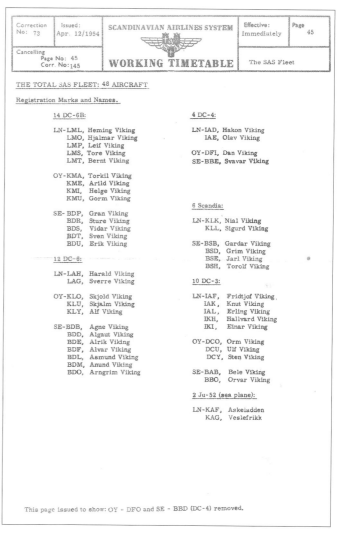

Correction No: 73	Issued: Apr. 12/1954	SCANDINAVIAN AIRLINES SYSTEM	Effective: Immediately	Page 45
Cancelling Page No: 45 Corr. No: 145		WORKING TIMETABLE	The SAS Fleet	

THE TOTAL SAS FLEET: 48 AIRCRAFT

Registration Marks and Names.

14 DC-6B:

LN-LML, Heming Viking
   LMO, Hjalmar Viking
   LMP, Leif Viking
   LMS, Tore Viking
   LMT, Bernt Viking

OY-KMA, Torkil Viking
   KME, Arild Viking
   KMI, Helge Viking
   KMU, Gorm Viking

SE-BDP, Gran Viking
   BDR, Sture Viking
   BDS, Vidar Viking
   BDT, Sven Viking
   BDU, Erik Viking

12 DC-6:

LN-LAH, Harald Viking
   LAG, Sverre Viking

OY-KLO, Skjold Viking
   KLU, Skjalm Viking
   KLY, Alf Viking

SE-BDB, Agne Viking
   BDD, Algaut Viking
   BDE, Alrik Viking
   BDF, Alvar Viking
   BDL, Asmund Viking
   BDM, Amund Viking
   BDO, Arngrim Viking

4 DC-4:

LN-IAD, Hakon Viking
   IAE, Olav Viking

OY-DFI, Dan Viking
SE-BBE, Svavar Viking

6 Scandia:

LN-KLK, Nial Viking
   KLL, Sigurd Viking

SE-BSB, Gardar Viking
   BSD, Grim Viking
   BSE, Jarl Viking
   BSH, Torolf Viking

10 DC-3:

LN-IAF, Fridtjof Viking
   IAK, Knut Viking
   IAL, Erling Viking
   IKH, Hallvard Viking
   IKI, Einar Viking

OY-DCO, Orm Viking
   DCU, Ulf Viking
   DCY, Sten Viking

SE-BAB, Bele Viking
   BBO, Orvar Viking

2 Ju-52 (sea plane):

LN-KAF, Askeladden
   KAG, Veslefrikk

This page issued to show: OY - DFO and SE - BBD (DC-4) removed.

In April 1954, the SAS fleet consisted of the long-range DC-4 and DC-6 and 6B, plus the SAAB 90 Scandia, Douglas DC-3, and even the Junkers Ju 52/3m for short- and medium-haul routes. The latter was operated on floats on routes along the Norwegian coast. *SAS / author's collection*

And they did so with full traffic rights from Germany. In 1954, for example, the Hanseatic cities of Hamburg and Bremen were en route stops for SAS North Atlantic routes to New York. Routes to Johannesburg in South Africa and Khartoum in Sudan also passed through Hamburg. SAS flights to South America, serving Recife, Rio de Janeiro, Montevideo, Buenos Aires, and Santiago de Chile, stopped off in Düsseldorf and Frankfurt, while only the Rhine-Main Airport was used by SAS aircraft en route to Southeast Asia, serving Karachi, Calcutta, Rangoon, Bangkok, Hong Kong, Manila, and Tokyo.

In the 1950s, SAS offered only first-class service on its long-haul routes, something that is unimaginable today. The Douglas DC-6Bs and DC-7Cs of the Royal Viking service were equipped with comfortable Dormette reclining seats and Pullman beds in berths in the rear of the cabin. For less well-heeled passengers, SAS alternatively offered a less expensive globetrotter tourist class on other aircraft of this type. Here, the highlight was that the seats were staggered. This meant that passengers had no direct contact with their neighbors, and therefore still had some privacy even with the more cramped seating conditions.

Even after the founding of the new Lufthansa in 1953 and the return of air sovereignty to the Federal Republic of Germany in 1955, SAS initially invoked the flight rights it had been granted by the occupying powers immediately after the end of the war. But in the second half of the 1950s, Hans-Christoph Seebohm, then West German minister of transport, urged SAS to gradually withdraw from Germany. This was in favor of the young, new Lufthansa. This step was finally taken in the early 1960s. By then, SAS had switched most of its intercontinental routes to direct flights from Copenhagen, gradually leaving the domestic German connections to Lufthansa, and established a partnership-based neighborly service with Lufthansa between Scandinavia and Germany. Until the 1970s, however, the flying Scandinavians continued to offer European destinations from Germany. For example, SAS Douglas DC-9s flew from Copenhagen via Stuttgart to Athens, Cairo, and Madrid.

SAS DOMESTIC GERMAN ROUTES FLOWN BY DC-3S IN THE 1950S:

Frankfurt–Düsseldorf
Frankfurt–Hamburg
Frankfurt–Stuttgart
Frankfurt–Munich
Bremen–Düsseldorf
Bremen– Hamburg
Düsseldorf–Stuttgart
Hamburg–Hanover
Hamburg–Stuttgart
Hanover–Stuttgart
Munich–Nuremberg
Munich–Stuttgart

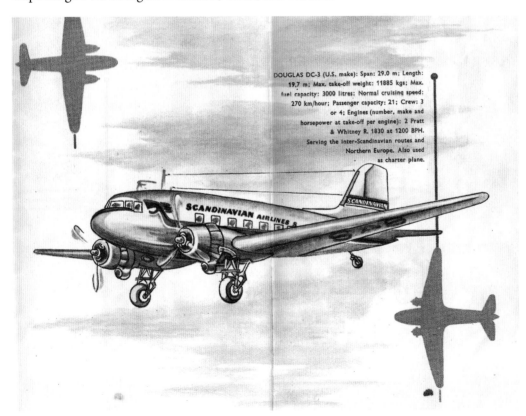

DOUGLAS DC-3 (U.S. make): Span: 29.0 m; Length: 19.7 m; Max. take-off weight: 11885 kgs; Max. fuel capacity: 3000 litres; Normal cruising speed: 270 km/hour; Passenger capacity: 21; Crew: 3 or 4; Engines (number, make and horsepower at take-off per engine): 2 Pratt & Whitney R. 1830 at 1200 BPH. Serving the Inter-Scandinavian routes and Northern Europe. Also used as charter plane.

Excerpt from a brochure published by SAS in the 1950s extolling the virtues of its fleet. *Author's collection*

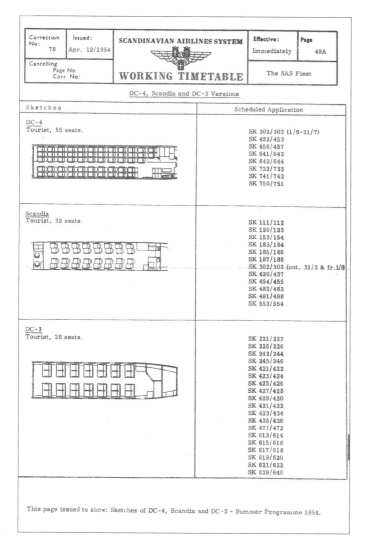

Correction No: 78	Issued: Apr. 12/1954	SCANDINAVIAN AIRLINES SYSTEM	Effective: Immediately	Page 49A
Cancelling Page No: Corr. No:		WORKING TIMETABLE	The SAS Fleet	

DC-4, Scandia and DC-3 Versions

Sketches	Scheduled Application
DC-4 Tourist, 55 seats.	SK 302/303 (1/6-31/7) SK 452/453 SK 456/457 SK 641/642 SK 643/644 SK 732/733 SK 741/742 SK 750/751
Scandia Tourist, 32 seats.	SK 111/112 SK 120/123 SK 153/154 SK 183/184 SK 185/186 SK 187/188 SK 302/303 (unt. 31/5 & fr.1/8) SK 420/437 SK 454/455 SK 482/483 SK 491/498 SK 553/554
DC-3 Tourist, 28 seats.	SK 221/222 SK 225/226 SK 243/244 SK 245/246 SK 421/422 SK 423/424 SK 425/426 SK 427/428 SK 429/430 SK 431/432 SK 433/434 SK 435/436 SK 471/472 SK 613/614 SK 615/616 SK 617/618 SK 619/620 SK 621/622 SK 639/640

This page issued to show: Sketches of DC-4, Scandia and DC-3 - Summer Programme 1954.

Comparison of the seating plans for the SAS DC-4, DC-3, and SAAB Scandia. *SAS / author's collection*

Top right: The Swedish airline ABA, one of the airlines that founded SAS, used postcards such as this one to advertise a flight aboard its DC-3s. The DC-3s of ABA, DNL, and DDL formed the basis of the fleet used by SAS in West Germany. *Author's collection*

Right: This aircraft on display at the Danish Museum of Technology in Elsinore is finished in the colors and has the cabin interior of a DC-3 of the Danish SAS parent company DDL. *Author's photo*

Left: The historical SAS logo is present on the fuselage of the DC-3 owned by the Flying Veterans Association of Sweden. *Author's photo*

Below: Every single rivet on the fuselage of "Fridtjof Viking," the DC-3 of the Flying Veterans, reveals itself in the light from the setting sun. *Author's photo*

Above: This postcard, issued by SAS founding carrier ABA—Swedish Airlines—shows the unusual placement of the DC-3 main entrance door on the right-hand side of the fuselage. *Author's collection*

Like SAS, the Swiss airline Swissair was one of the first airlines to regularly serve West German destinations after the end of the Second World War—here, Stuttgart Airport. *Author's collection*

SAS DC-3s also operated in Arctic conditions in the far north of Scandinavia. *SAS Museum, Oslo*

Founded in 1923, the Finnish national airline Aero OY has been operating under the name "Finnair" since 1953. Its DC-3, registration OH-LCH, arrived in Copenhagen on a scheduled flight from Helsinki on June 10, 1966, where it was photographed by Tom Weihe. *Tom Weihe*

The historic OH-LCH is still airworthy and is operated as a flying museum by the Airveteran Association. *Lassi Tolvanen / Airveteran*

This DC-3, registration OH-VKB, operated by Finnish airline Karair, was originally flown by Sweden's AB Aerotransport (ABA) and SAS before moving to neighboring Finland. It is now part of the collection of the Finnish Aviation Museum at Helsinki-Vantaa. *Tom Weihe*

Faeroe Airways was an airline based on the Faeroe Islands in the North Atlantic that flew DC-3s to Copenhagen and other destinations. This photo of one of its aircraft, built in 1943 and registered OY-DNP, was taken there on December 27, 1966. The aircraft was irreparably damaged in a ground accident in Copenhagen on October 17, 1967, and subsequently scrapped there. *Tom Weihe*

DC-3 SE-CFW of the short-lived Swedish airline Hilair. It still wears the livery of its previous owner, Austrian Airlines. It ended up in a Belgian children's playground before being scrapped. *Tom Weihe*

CHAPTER 8
AROUND THE WORLD WITH THE DC-3

A SELECTION OF DC-3S THAT
CONTINUED FLYING IN EUROPE
AND THE UNITED STATES OVER
THE PAST DECADES

DOUGLAS DC-3 DDA CLASSIC AIRLINES, THE NETHERLANDS

The DC-3 operated by DDA Classic Airlines was originally produced as a military C-47 in 1943 with the construction number 19754. It served with the US Army Air Force (USAAF) until 1961. After temporary storage at the Military Aircraft Storage and Disposition Center in Arizona, this Skytrain was used by the US Federal Aviation Administration (FAA) for a few months in 1964 before Somali Airlines flew it from the United States to the Somali capital of Mogadishu in May 1964.

DDA Classic Airlines of the Netherlands offers nostalgia flights from Amsterdam-Schiphol in its DC-3, which was built in 1947. *DDA Airlines*

For many years the Congo Queen, owned by Åke Jansson of Sweden, was a frequent guest at European airshows. Sold to buyers in China, it now flies in the historical colors of the China National Aviation Corporation. *Author's photo*

Further stops for this aviation old-timer were Malta and Egypt before it was acquired by the Dutch aviation enthusiasts of DDA Classic Airlines. Between 1987 and 1999, they put in thousands of hours restoring the aircraft. Originally painted in the historical colors of Dutch airlines KLM and Martinair (Martin Air Charter), this DC-3 now has a neutral livery for trips to air shows and for sightseeing flights. DDA Classic Airlines is based at Amsterdam-Schiphol Airport.

DOUGLAS C-47B-35-DK CONGO QUEEN

Although ordered by the US Army Air Force (USAAF) in 1944 as a C-47B-35-DK, this aircraft was delivered to the Royal Air Force a year later. It arrived in England on June 22, after its first Atlantic crossing. Just one year later, the C-47 was given to the Royal Canadian Air Force (RCAF). Again, the aircraft crossed the Atlantic—this time in the opposite direction en route to Canada. In 1977, the RCAF sold the veteran, last used as a radar trainer, to the aircraft dealer Basler Air Service, where it was discovered by Åke Jansson of Sweden. At the time, he was looking for an aircraft for transport duties in the West African nation of Zaire. With the adventurous Jansson at the controls, the DC-3 crossed the Atlantic for the third time, this time to Africa, where it served as a freighter and passenger aircraft for many years. After political unrest in Africa, Åke Jansson finally returned with the DC-3 to his native Sweden. For many years, the Dakota was based at his private airfield near Stockholm. In 2015, it received the American civil registration N41CQ, but then the US authorities grounded the aircraft, and apart from a brief respite in the summer of 2017, this was not lifted until the summer of 2018. But then the Swedish aviation agency refused to certify the aircraft, and it was sold to China in 2019. There it continues to fly in the historical colors of the China National Aviation Corporation.

DOUGLAS DC-3, ASSOCIATION FRANCE DC-3, FRANCE

This French-registered DC-3 was originally produced as a military C-47 in 1948 with construction number 9172. The purchase price paid by the US Army Air Force was $109,663. After the end of World War II, and its temporary retirement from military service, the C-47 was converted into a civilian DC-3 by Scottish Aviation in the United Kingdom. Between 1948 and 1950, during the Berlin Airlift, this Dakota served as a so-called raisin bomber, transporting vital supplies to the trapped population of West Berlin. The eventful history of this DC-3 continued with renewed military use in Great Britain and France before it became the private aircraft of the self-proclaimed emperor of the Central African Republic, Jean Bedel Bokassa, in 1975. It was not until 1983 that it returned to Europe after being purchased by France's Transvalair, flying courier shipments for express service DHL, among others. With the help of the French domestic airline Air Inter, the France DC-3 Association finally acquired this elderly veteran with an eventful history, which has been lovingly maintained and displayed at air shows ever since.

The Association France DC-3 operates this veteran, which was built in 1948. *France DC-3*

The DC-3 of the Danish Dakota Friends was previously operated by the US Air Force, the Norwegian air force, and the Scandinavian airline SAS. *DC-3 Vennerne*

DC-3 VENNERNE, DENMARK

After serving with the US Army Air Force, the Norwegian air force, Scandinavian Airlines System (SAS), and the Danish air force as a VIP aircraft, the group "Danish Dakota Friends" acquired this sprightly old-timer in 1992. The aircraft left the Douglas factory in Long Beach, California, on April 3, 1944. Today the aircraft is based on an airfield near the Danish capital, Copenhagen, and is flown for the benefit of club members within Europe.

SOUTH COAST AIRWAYS, GREAT BRITAIN

After its completion in 1943, this Douglas C-47 was delivered to the US Army Air Force. Its first area of operation in World War II was North Africa. In February 1944, the USAAF transferred the Dakota to Europe. After the end of the war, it was sold to the Czech airline CSA in 1946. From then on, the aircraft flew in the airline's passenger service as a civilian DC-3. Further stations in the eventful life of this old-timer were the French navy (1958–1983) and the French airlines Stellair and Transvallair. In 1994, the British Dakota specialist Air Atlantique bought her and mothballed the aircraft until it was taken over by South Coast Airways in 1996. It was subsequently used mainly to show Dakota fans and tourists visiting London the sights of the British capital from the air. South Coast Airways ceased operations in 2002. Four years later, G-DAKK was airlifted to Lelystad, Holland, where it was dismantled and transported to the Dutch Overloon War Museum as a static World War II exhibit.

DOUGLAS DC-3 (C-47) N1944A

The DC-3 with the American registration N1944A was built as a C-47A and was sent to the European front for use by the US Army Air Force immediately after its completion in 1944. There, it served as a glider tug and drop plane for parachutists, among other duties, from Great Britain. At the end of the war, it returned to Europe after a brief interlude in the United States. Its operational base was initially the USAAF base at Wiesbaden in Hesse. From there, it most likely saw action as a "raisin bomber" during the Berlin Airlift in 1948 and 1949.

In 1950, the US Air Force sold the C-47 to the Norwegian air force, in whose service the aircraft was based at Oslo-Gardermoen. From 1956, after being sold to the Danish air force, it was based at Vaerloese, near Copenhagen. In 1974, the DC-3 was converted by the Danish Atomic Energy Commission to serve as a special aircraft for measuring air pollution. After its retirement from Danish military service, the Douglas transport was initially parked at Vaerloese until American aviation enthusiasts discovered it in 1983 and took it to the United States. In 1997, the current British owners finally acquired this aged flying old-timer, which in 1999—fifty-five years after its maiden flight—once again made the journey from the United States to Great Britain. This was already the third Atlantic crossing for this DC-3. But one more was to follow, because today the aircraft is part of the aviation collection of Kermit Weeks in Florida.

The Flygande Veteraner's C-47A-60-DL Skytrain played an active role in the airborne landing operations over Normandy on D-day, June 6, 1944, with the serial number 330732. *Author's photo*

DOUGLAS DC-3 AIR ATLANTIQUE, GREAT BRITAIN

The DC-3 operated by Air Atlantique left the Douglas production line at Santa Monica, California, in 1943. Originally built as a C-47 with the construction number 26569, it initially served with the US Army Air Force. Soon after its arrival in Europe, the aircraft was transferred to the RAF, which used it as a glider tug over Normandy and the Netherlands.

After the war ended, this Dakota with the RAF serial KK116 took part in the Berlin Airlift in 1948 and 1949, helping to ensure the freedom and survival of the population of West Berlin. In civilian life, this aircraft was flown as a passenger aircraft in Great Britain, Iceland, Jordan, and the United States. Air Atlantique purchased the aircraft in 1981 and used it for carrying passengers and freight, and for combating oil spills off the Welsh coast and around the Shetland Islands. After Air Atlantique was bought out, the aircraft was stationed on the Isle of Man.

FLYGANDE VETERANER, SWEDEN

Delivered to the US Army Air Force on October 5, 1943, by the Douglas Aircraft Company in Long Beach, the C-47 A-60-DL Skytrain with serial 330732 played an active role in the D-day airborne operations over Normandy on June 6, 1944. After retirement from military service, it was converted from a C-47 into a DC-3C by Canadair Ltd. in 1946. Part of the package was the replacement of the large cargo doors in the rear with a smaller passenger-boarding door, sound insulation, and the installation of comfortable passenger seats. After being purchased by the Norwegian carrier DNL, one of the SAS parent companies, the DC-3C came to Europe and operated on the SAS route network from 1948 to 1957 with the name Fridtjof Viking and registration LN-IAF. After DNL was sold to ABA, a Swedish airline that also had a stake in SAS, ABA operated the aircraft with the Swedish registration SE-CFP at Linjeflyg, a subsidiary of SAS within Sweden. In 1960, the aircraft was sold with the Swedish military type designation Tp 79 to the Scandinavian country's air force, which flew it until 1982. In 1983, it was acquired by Ingemar Wärme and Jimmie Berglund, who founded the Flygande Veteraner Association to operate the flying old-timer. On June 26, 1984, the DC-3 regained its original Swedish civil registration. Given the name "Daisy," it has since flown again as SE-CFP. The club, which is still very active today, is financed by members' annual dues and sponsor donations.

BATTLE OF BRITAIN MEMORIAL FLIGHT, ROYAL AIR FORCE, GREAT BRITAIN

The aircraft was built in 1942, and after serving with the US Army Air Force and the Royal Canadian Air Force, in 1972 it was sold to the Royal Aircraft Establishment at Farnborough. There it was used for a variety of tasks, including the dropping of sonobuoys and remotely piloted aerial vehicles.

In 1993, the aircraft became the property of the Royal Air Force, with the serial number ZA947, and the veteran was assigned to the Battle of Britain Memorial Flight. This unit maintains aircraft types flown by the RAF in World War II in flying condition, and they regularly participate in air shows, mainly in Great Britain. Among the types flown by the flight are the iconic Spitfire fighter and Lancaster bomber.

Since 1993 the Royal Air
Force's Battle of Britain
Memorial Flight has
maintained this Dakota, along
with a Spitfire (*foreground*)
and an Avro Lancaster
bomber, in flying condition.
*Author's photo (top);
Hamburg Airport (bottom)*

CHAPTER 9
COMPETING PROPELLER-DRIVEN AIRLINERS FROM THE EARLY DAYS OF THE DC-3

JUNKERS JU 52/3M

Manufacturer: Junkers, Germany
Passengers: 16
Wingspan: 96 ft.
Length: 62 ft.
Height: 20 ft.
Power plant: 3 Pratt & Whitney PW1340
    S1 H1Gs
Max. takeoff weight: 25,572 lbs.
Cruise: 118 mph
Max. range: 512 mi.
Crew: 3 in cockpit, 1 in cabin
Note: Figures for D-AQUI of the
Deutsche Lufthansa Berlin Foundation

Scandinavian was an Eldorado for Junkers Ju 52/3m floatplanes. Among the operators of commercial aircraft on floats was the Swedish airline ABA. *SAS Museum, Oslo*

The Ju 52/3m operated by the Norwegian airline DNL docked in the port of the Swedish metropolis of Göteborg (Gothenburg). The aircraft pictured here is the "Auntie Ju" that Lufthansa operated as a heritage aircraft until a few years ago. *SAS*

The Ju 52/3m in its later incarnation as property of the Lufthansa Berlin Foundation prior to its flight from the United States to Germany in 1986. *Lufthansa*

In 1929, Hugo Junkers commissioned his chief designer, Dipl.-Ing. Ernst Zindel, to design a single-engine cargo aircraft. The inspiration behind this decision was a report by leading employees of the former Junkers Luftverkehrs, which merged with Deutsche Aero Lloyd to form Deutsche Luft Hansa in 1926. They saw freight traffic in particular as a lucrative area of business, for which the Ju 52, which had a cabin capacity of 692 cubic feet, was tailor-made.

When the first aircraft took to the skies on September 11, 1930, it had little in common with its later sisters of the same type. The prototype had a single engine mounted in the nose, a liquid-cooled, twelve-cylinder BMW VII aU producing 690 hp for takeoff with a continuous maximum power rating of 600 hp. At the time, this was the most powerful aircraft engine made in Germany. It powered a four-blade propeller via a reduction gearbox, which gave the aircraft a cruising speed of a full 99.4 mph. The Ju 52/1m could carry a maximum payload of 4,012 lbs. over a distance of 621 miles.

Large loading hatches, including one in the cabin roof, were supposed to ease the loading of bulky cargoes. In order to make the aircraft appealing as a passenger aircraft, Zindel had conceived a three-engine version of the Ju 52 from the very beginning. The path to the Ju 52/3m took concrete shape in April 1931, when a Ju 52/1m was fitted with mockups of two wing engines for drag tests.

The first Ju 52/3m, equipped with three Pratt & Whitney Hornet radial engines, flew on March 7, 1932. Serial number 4008 was destined for the Lloyd Aero Boliviano airline and did not yet meet the series standard of later aircraft. Only many further aerodynamic improvements, such as engine and landing-gear fairings, increased the top speed of the subsequent Ju 52/3m from an initial figure of 146 mph—to a maximum of 196 mph.

Like the American DC-3, the Junkers Ju 52/3m became a sales success. In the period before the start of World War II, Junkers sold more than 400 aircraft to airlines around the world. The robust "Auntie Jus" flew reliably on Lufthansa's European route network, but also on routes over the South American Andes, in icy Siberia, and on expeditionary flights from Germany to destinations as distant as China.

93

This historical painting showing the destinations served by the Ju 52 is taken from the brochure *10 Jahre Deutsche Lufthansa* ("Ten years of Deutsche Lufthansa") from the year 1936. *Author's collection*

Imposing size comparison between the Ju 52 and a Boeing 747. *Lufthansa*

After the National Socialists came to power and began rearming Germany, the Junkers Werke received orders for mass production of the Ju 52 as an interim bomber. Following the example of the American automobile industry, a final assembly production line was created. Over the course of the Second World War, other manufacturers produced components and even complete aircraft under license. In addition to German companies such as Blohm & Voss and Weser Flugzeugwerke, foreign manufacturers also took part in production of the Ju 52. Two companies continued producing the "Auntie Ju" even after the war. In France, Amiot built approximately 150 Ju 52/3m aircraft, which it designated the AAC.1. CASA, now the Spanish Airbus partner, produced 170 examples of the Ju 52/3m as the Casa 352.

In addition to the military transports flown by the air arms of France, Spain, and Switzerland, a variety of airlines operated the civil Ju 52/3m as a passenger aircraft after the war, including Air France and British European Airways. In northern Europe, Scandinavian Airlines System (SAS) operated the Ju 52/3m on floats, serving towns along the coast of Norway. One of the former SAS Ju 52s flew for many years as the Lufthansa Berlin Foundation's D-AQUI.

D-AQUI: THE MOST FAMOUS "AUNTIE JU" OF THEM ALL

For many years this aircraft was known as D-AQUI. And even if that Junkers Ju 52/3m of the Deutsche Lufthansa Berlin Foundation can no longer be admired in the skies, the memory of the sonorous hum of its engines and its corrugated sheet metal skin lives on among many enthusiasts to this day.

Its life as an aircraft began officially on April 10, 1936, when Lufthansa christened it "Fritz Simon." But after a short time, Lufthansa parted with its "Auntie Ju" and sold her to the Norwegian airline Det Norske Luftfartselskap Fred. Olsen & Bergenske A/S (DNL). With its new registration LN-DAH and name "Falken" (Falcon), the young lady flew daily from south to north and north to south along the Norwegian coastline. DNL's Ju 52s served almost the same port cities as its maritime competitors—first and foremost the legendary mail steamers of the Hurtigruten (coastal express line). In 1938, the airline's route network stretched from Oslo all the way up to Kirkenes in Lapland, near the Russian border.

After the German invasion of Norway on April 9, 1940, many DNL employees fled to Great Britain or the United States. The aircraft remained in the country,

In this photo, the Deutsche Lufthansa Berlin Foundation's "Auntie Ju" shows off her corrugated-metal covering, shimmering in the sunlight. *Lufthansa*

however, and so LN-DAH returned to Lufthansa, which gave it back its original registration D-AQUI but now named it "Kurt Wintgens."

Even after the end of the war, the now-somewhat-aged "Ju" remained in Norway and returned to coastal flying under the Norwegian flag. Registered LN-KAF in May 1946, the aircraft was given its fourth name, "Askeladden" (a character in many Norwegian folktales). Reliable as she had been since her first days of service, LN-KAF flew for DNL until airline technicians discovered significant corrosion damage during a routine inspection in 1947. Only by combining the original LN-KAF, serial number 5489, with the fuselage and other components of a military Ju

52/3mg8e, serial number 130714, was the aircraft saved from imminent retirement. In February 1948, the new "Askeladden" took to the air again—now in the colors of the Scandinavian Airlines System (SAS), founded by DNL, the Swedish airline ABA/SILA, and the Danish carrier DDL on August 1, 1946. It was not until 1956 that SAS finally retired its tried-and-tested Ju 52s, two of which were still in service—including one that became D-AQUI of the Deutsche Lufthansa Berlin Foundation.

After its retirement, the fate of the Ju 52, as so often in its history, was initially on a knife edge. Plans to put it on display in a Norwegian museum fell through due to the Junkers' sheer size—and so SAS continued its search for a buyer. One was finally found in early 1957 in the form of the Ecuadorian company Transportes Aéreos Orientales S.A. Safely packed in twenty wooden crates, and accompanied by 20 tons of vital spare parts, the former LN-KAF arrived in South America in the summer of 1957. During unloading, she fell into the harbor, fortunately without suffering any major damage. This was one of the Ju 52's last encounters with the liquid element, since it was fitted with a wheeled undercarriage and henceforth flew as a land-based aircraft. Under the direction of the former Lufthansa pilot Christof Drexel, who had already arranged the purchase in Norway, the Ju 52 was assembled in Ecuador in the summer of 1957.

It was the beginning of a new era in the life of the aircraft, which is now known as the "Berlin-Tempelhof." It received the registration HC-ABS and the name "Amazonas." In 1962, the "Auntie Ju" was finally taken out of service after 8,000 hours of flying time, and henceforth it languished on the outskirts of Quito Airport, largely ignored. For eight years, the Junkers' corrugated sheet metal was left unprotected against the elements until the American Lester F. Weaver, a former bomber pilot, recognized the historical value of the "good old Auntie Ju" and acquired the vintage aircraft for 5,000 US dollars. After its aeronautical overhaul, the Ju 52, now registered with the initials of its new owner, N130LW, took off in October 1970 for an eight-day ferry flight to Illinois. Due to technical concerns, however, the US Federal Aviation Administration (FAA) granted only a restricted "Experimental" certification. After just two more years and another change of ownership, the Junkers finally passed into the hands of American aviation and science fiction author Martin Caidin for $52,500. Asked about his motives for buying it, his telling reply survives: "I just had to buy the damned plane!" In 1976, Caidin had his "Auntie Ju," now christened "Iron Annie," completely overhauled in Florida, a process that took about half a year and cost the proud Junkers owner almost a quarter of a million dollars. During this inspection, which went far beyond the usual, the Junkers' original BMW engines (a

license-built version of the Pratt & Whitney 1340) were replaced by Pratt & Whitney PW1340 S1 H1G Wasps, and it was fitted with wheels and brakes from a Curtiss C-46 Commando. Freshly overhauled, freshly painted, and given the fitting new registration N52JU, for the next eight years the corrugated metal airplane was the star of the American aviation old-timer scene.

The Junkers Ju 52/3m, serial number 130714, would perhaps have remained so to this day had it not been for the sixtieth anniversary of the "old" Lufthansa in 1986, which prompted the executive board of the "new" Lufthansa to look for an aircraft that, like no other, symbolized safety, efficiency, and engineering under the sign of the crane.

There was great joy among all Lufthansa employees when the crew of the "Iron Annie" landed her safely and happily at Hamburg-Fuhlsbüttel on December 28, 1984, after an extremely adventurous ferry flight. Once again, "good old Auntie Ju" had proven that she would not abandon her crew even in the most-adverse weather conditions and with critical technical problems. The two-week ferry flight covered almost 5,000 miles, from Grandpa Locka in sunny Florida, across wintry Labrador and icy Greenland, along the snowy Icelandic glaciers, through the Scottish and British rain, and all the way to Hamburg.

The Lufthansa Technik management at the time had estimated 6,000 man-hours to overhaul the aircraft, but wherever the experts took a closer look under the corrugated sheet metal skin of the "Auntie Ju," they discovered serious corrosion. In the summer of 1985, Lufthansa management initially pulled the proverbial plug because the budget had been far exceeded. But the top Lufthansa officials quickly succumbed to the charm of the now-elderly lady and cleared the way for all the necessary work to be done, right up to restoring her to airworthy condition.

In April 1986, the time had finally come. The proud "Ju" team was able to celebrate the certification of the rebuilt Junkers with the official registration D-CDLH in the highest Class 1 certification for passenger transport. The team even succeeded in obtaining the official blessing for the large-scale painting of the aircraft as the historic D-AQUI—although this registration no longer has any significance under aviation law. The valid registration is discreetly written in smaller letters on both sides of the fuselage, hidden under the tailplane.

On April 6, 1986, fifty years to the day after the first D-AQUI's maiden flight at Dessau, D-CDLH was christened "Berlin-Tempelhof." That legendary airport, which was the original Lufthansa's hub in the days of the Ju 52, corresponds to the importance of Frankfurt/Main to today's Lufthansa. In April 2019, the Lufthansa Executive Board decided to end the operation of historical aircraft within the group—and thus also the end for the D-AQUI. Today, the "Auntie Ju" is in storage at Paderborn Airport, waiting for better times.

Apart from Lufthansa, the Danish carrier DDL was the only airline to receive the commercial version of the Focke-Wulf Fw 200. The outbreak of war prevented further deliveries to interested airlines. *Author's collection*

FOCKE-WULF FW 200 CONDOR

Manufacturer: Focke-Wulf Flugzeugbau, Germany
Maiden flight: July 27, 1937
Passengers: 25
Wingspan: 107.7 ft.
Length: 78.25 ft.
Height: 19.7 ft.
Power plant: 4 BMW 132 G radial engines, each producing 720 hp
Cruise: approx. 205 mph.
Range: 901 miles
Crew: 2 in the cockpit, 2 in the cabin
Note: Specification for the Fw 200 KA-1 civil version

„Vergebens, mein Lieber!
Wir fliegen auch mit zwei Motoren ruhig weiter."

This contemporaneous postcard published by Lufthansa in the 1930s was intended to illustrate the flight safety of the Fw 200 Condor—even when the devil caused two of its four engines to fail. *Author's collection*

stresses to which the aircraft structure was subjected: after landing in New York, the crew initially tried in vain to open the cabin door of the Fw 200. The cause was quickly determined to be that the fuselage had twisted due to the weight of the auxiliary tanks installed in the cabin! And yet, the successful flight by D-ACON across the Atlantic to New York had proven that large land-based aircraft could also conquer oceans. And they could do so with much-lower structural weights and costs than flying boats with their heavy boat hulls.

A MODERN LONG-RANGE AIRCRAFT

At the height of the seaplane era, a land-based aircraft made a splash with a spectacular record-breaking flight across the North Atlantic that paved the way for today's long-haul air transport. It was August 10, 1938, when the elegant Focke-Wulf Fw 200 Condor with the registration D-ACON taxied into takeoff position at Berlin-Staaken Airport. The destination of the nonstop flight piloted by Lufthansa flight captain Henke: New York. A total of 3,958 miles lay ahead of the crew and their aircraft, which was equipped with additional fuel tanks for this epic flight. The chosen route took them over Hamburg, Glasgow, Newfoundland, and Halifax at a cruising altitude of 6,500 feet to Floyd Bennett Airport in the US East Coast metropolis. An enthusiastic crowd welcomed the Atlantic fliers to American soil after a flying time of twenty-four hours, thirty-six minutes, and twelve seconds. Although not originally designed for such great distances, the elegant Condor proved its worth on this pioneering flight. The following episode illustrates the

THE CHAMPAGNE WAGER

The development team around Kurt Tank, technical director of the Focke-Wulf Flugzeugwerke, was firmly convinced that the future of long-haul air travel belonged to fast land-based aircraft. Just one year would pass until the maiden flight of the Fw 200, which was designed strictly according to Lufthansa's specifications and commissioned by the airline. That was why Kurt Tank and Lufthansa director Carl-August Baron von Gablenz wagered twenty-five bottles of champagne. Tank's small, well-trained, and highly motivated development team set about making the Condor. In the end, the Focke-Wulf team took eleven days longer than promised to deliver the maiden flight by the Fw 200 V1. Gritting his teeth, Tank sent the champagne to Baron von Gablenz—but immediately received an identical number of bottles from his betting partner. The performance of the Focke-Wulf team was so exceptional that the Lufthansa director did not care that the aircraft had made its maiden flight eleven days later than promised.

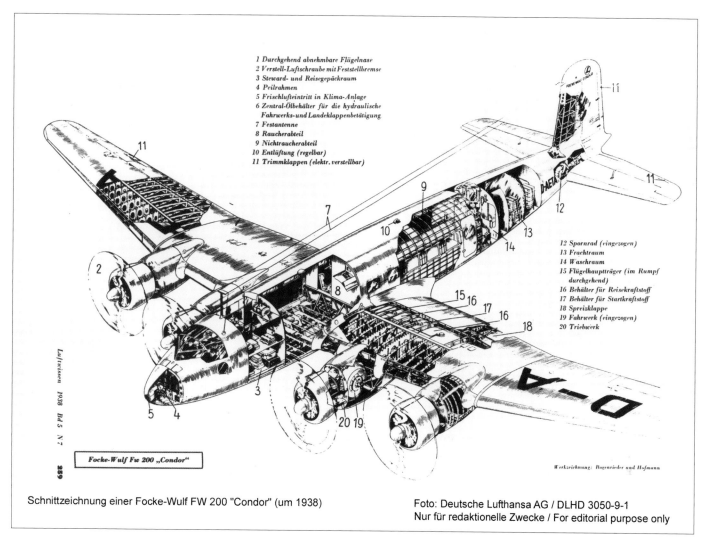

1 *Durchgehend abnehmbare Flügelnase*
2 *Verstell-Luftschraube mit Feststellbremse*
3 *Steward- und Reisegepäckraum*
4 *Peilrahmen*
5 *Frischlufteintritt in Klima-Anlage*
6 *Zentral-Ölbehälter für die hydraulische*
  Fahrwerks- und Landeklappenbetätigung
7 *Festantenne*
8 *Raucherabteil*
9 *Nichtraucherabteil*
10 *Entlüftung (regelbar)*
11 *Trimmklappen (elektr. verstellbar)*

12 *Spornrad (eingezogen)*
13 *Frachtraum*
14 *Waschraum*
15 *Flügelhauptträger (im Rumpf*
   durchgehend)
16 *Behälter für Reisekraftstoff*
17 *Behälter für Startkraftstoff*
18 *Spreizklappe*
19 *Fahrwerk (eingezogen)*
20 *Triebwerk*

Luftreisen 1938 Bd 5 N 7

289

Focke-Wulf Fw 200 „Condor"

Werkzeichnung: Rogenrieder und Hofmann

Schnittzeichnung einer Focke-Wulf FW 200 "Condor" (um 1938)

Foto: Deutsche Lufthansa AG / DLHD 3050-9-1
Nur für redaktionelle Zwecke / For editorial purpose only

On July 27, 1937, the Fw 200 V1 prototype took off from Bremen, crewed by Kurt Tank and chief test pilot Hans Sander. In scheduled service, the Condor provided reliable service within Europe and elsewhere, and not only for Lufthansa. Other aircraft were operated by the Brazilian airline Syndicato Condor and the Danish carrier Det Danske Luftfartselskab A/S (DDL). Sales to other interested parties, such as the Dutch airline KLM and the Finnish Aero O/Y, were thwarted by the outbreak of World War II. With a maximum range of 900

This cutaway drawing of a Lufthansa Fw 200 Condor, produced circa 1938, reveals the modern structure of the aircraft's airframe. *Lufthansa*

miles, the Fw 200 was by no means a long-range aircraft, even if the spectacular nonstop flight to New York or the sensational demonstration flight from Berlin to Tokyo might suggest otherwise. Rather, the Fw 200 was a reliable medium-range passenger aircraft and, as such, was successfully operated by Lufthansa and the Danish airline DDL.

RECOVERED FROM THE SEA

In 1981, the remains of a wartime Fw 200 were located in a fjord near Trondheim, Norway. Experts quickly recognized the value of the wrecked aircraft. The remains of a Focke-Wulf Fw 200 were a true rarity—no other aircraft of this type was known to exist! The aircraft had been ditched in February 1942 due to a technical defect and had been lying at a depth of over 197 feet ever since. In return for the restoration of a Ju 52/3m for a Norwegian museum by a team of Lufthansa enthusiasts, the aircraft was obtained for the German Museum of Technology in Berlin. Salvage operations proved complicated, however, since corrosion had progressed further than underwater examinations had suggested.

When it was set down on the salvage platform on May 26, 1999, the Condor wreck broke up. Nevertheless, the involved partners decided to tackle the complex restoration project. The Deutsche Lufthansa Berlin Foundation, together with the German Museum of Technology in Berlin, Airbus in Bremen, and Rolls-Royce Germany at the Oberursel plant, set themselves the goal of transforming the badly damaged aircraft back into a respectable piece of commercial aircraft history. And the feat was accomplished—the world's only completely preserved Fw 200 Condor is now on display in a hangar at the former Berlin-Tempelhof Airport, gleaming as if it had just left the Focke-Wulf final assembly hall!

CURTISS C-46 COMMANDO

Manufacturer: Curtiss-Wright, Buffalo, New York
First flight: March 26, 1940
Number built: 3,181
Wingspan: 108 ft.
Length: 76.3 ft.
Height: 21.6 ft.
Power plant: 2 Pratt & Whitney R-2800 Double Wasp radial
    engines
Cruise: approx. 185 mph
Range: approx. 1,240 miles
Crew: 2

DIRECT COMPETITOR TO THE DC-3

The Curtiss C-46 was designed to carry large quantities of cargo in the underfloor cargo holds as well as on the main deck. For this purpose, it was given an optimally shaped, "waisted" fuselage with two circular segments set one above the other, analogous to the Boeing Stratocruiser or the Vickers Vanguard. Viewed from the front, this large-volume fuselage cross section looks like an upside-down "8." This means that the C-46 is not as elegant as its contemporary the Douglas DC-3, but it can carry almost twice the payload at a higher altitude. In addition to carrying cargo, the design, initially designated the CW-20, was also designed to carry passengers, forty of whom could be seated comfortably aboard the Commando.

In service with the US Air Force, the US Navy, and the US Marine Corps, the C-46 proved itself on every front in World War II and was even used by the CIA in the Vietnam War until the early 1970s. After their military careers ended, numerous Commandos were taken over by airlines, which used them as freighters or passenger aircraft. Among them was Deutsche Lufthansa, which leased Curtiss C-46s from American airlines for transporting cargo in the 1960s. To this day, many of these aircraft have proven their worth in daily service and under the most-difficult climatic conditions—including in the North American Arctic.

Both Lufthansa of Germany and SAS of Scandinavia operated leased examples of the Curtiss C-46 Commando in the early postwar years. *Lufthansa (top); author's collection (right)*

The cockpit of the Curtiss C-46D Commando on display in the World War II gallery of the National Museum of the United States Air Force. *Ken La Rock, US Air Force photo*

CHAPTER 10
THE BEST REPLACEMENT FOR A DC-3 IS A . . . ?

Many aircraft makers have tried their hand at bringing a type to market that was planned as a replacement for the indestructible ones. The following is a small selection of the countless types. Some of them were successful, but most of them were only hopefuls that failed to live up to expectations.

SAAB 90 SCANDIA

Manufacturer: Svenska Aeroplan Aktiebolaget (SAAB), Linköping, Sweden
First flight: November 16, 1946
Number built: 18
Wingspan: 91.8 ft.
Length: 69.9 ft.
Height: 23.3 ft.
Power plant: 2 Pratt & Whitney R-2180E-1 Twin Wasp radial engines
Cruise: approx. 242 mph
Range: 1,491 miles
Crew: 2 in the cockpit, 1 in the cabin
Note: Data for SAS version

The SAAB Scandia was a beacon of hope for the Swedish aviation industry, which hoped to market a successor to the DC-3. A final assembly line was set up at Fokker in Holland especially for this purpose, after SAAB was forced to use its own production capacity for military aircraft. However, a total of just nineteen aircraft were built in Sweden and the Netherlands. SAS

THE NEW HOPE

At a Christmas dinner in 1943, Carl Florman, director of the Swedish airline AB Aerotransport (ABA), and Ragnar Wahrgren, director of SAAB Aircraft Works, first discussed the possibility of building a commercial airliner in Sweden. Florman was looking for a modern aircraft type with which to launch his airline ABA in the anticipated peacetime. Since SAAB had never built such a large commercial aircraft and also had no experience whatsoever in the civil aviation business, ABA, which had been active since 1926, provided the ideal development partner. On February 23, 1944, SAAB presented its first concept ideas, which met ABA's basic expectations for the layout of the new airliner in all respects. The low-wing monoplane with retractable landing gear was to be powered by two Pratt & Whitney R-1830 Twin Wasp engines, which ABA hoped would provide synergies in engine overhaul with the airline's DC-3 fleet. Florman also wanted an all-metal aircraft with a capacity of twenty-five to thirty passengers plus cargo, a range of 621 miles, a cruising speed of 186 mph, and a maximum takeoff weight of 25,574 lbs.

Only five days later, the SAAB Supervisory Board approved production of the hitherto unnamed project. Although ABA provided massive engineering support for what was now internally called the "Civilt Trafikflygplan" (civil airliner), the airline was initially reluctant to place orders. However, this did not stop SAAB from proceeding with the project as planned. A six-month strike in the Swedish metal industry and the complex development work delayed the first flight of the aircraft, now officially called the SAAB 90 Scandia, which had originally been scheduled for 1945. Thus, the SE-BCA registered prototype did not take off for its uneventful maiden flight until November 16, 1946, at Linköping. One result of subsequent flight tests was that the production aircraft were fitted with more-powerful Pratt & Whitney R-2180 engines. In March 1947, a demonstration aircraft took off on a sales tour of Europe, but to the great disappointment of SAAB management, it failed to result in a single order.

It was not until April 20, 1948, that AB Aerotransport became the first customer to sign an order for ten examples of the production version, the SAAB 90A-2. Two years later, the Brazilian airlines VASP and Aerovias do Brasil followed with an order for an initial six SAAB 90s. Following the take-over of Aerovias by VASP on December 21, 1950, the Scandia delivery positions were also transferred to VASP. These Latin American orders were preceded by a sales tour of the US and South America with the SAAB 90 prototype, but the two Brazilian airlines were the only ones to show any interest.

After a ferry flight that took it from Sweden to Rio de Janeiro via Geneva, Lisbon, Dakar, and Recife, the first aircraft was delivered to VASP in June 1950. ABA, by then part of Scandinavian Airlines (SAS), took delivery of its first Scandia in October 1950, having previously reduced its order by four aircraft to a total of six SAAB 90s.

In 1951, the Swedish air force gave SAAB the choice of either ceasing Scandia production altogether or moving it to another location. The reason was the planned expansion of the Swedish air force by ten additional squadrons and their equipment, with 661 SAAB J29 Tunnan fighters ordered from SAAB. The Scandia stood in the way of their production at SAAB's Linköping plant—but a solution presented itself in the form of a transfer of SAAB 90 production to Fokker in Amsterdam. This was preceded by unsuccessful negotiations with the Italian Fiat Group. On May 2, 1952, Fokker and SAAB contractually agreed to supply components from Sweden and to have SAAB 90 final assembly in Holland. However, the SAAB 90 was also a foreign entity in Amsterdam, because at the same time Fokker was busy building up production facilities for its own F-27 Friendship. Since a transfer of Scandia production back to Sweden did not seem economically justifiable, SAAB of necessity ceased all sales efforts. Thus, in September 1954, Fokker delivered the eighteenth Scandia produced in Sweden and Holland. This SAAB 90, with the registration SE-BSL and destined for SAS, marked the end of production of this aircraft type. SAS retired its last Scandia in the second half of 1957 and sold its entire fleet to VASP. In Brazil, however, SAAB 90s remained in active airline service until July 22, 1969.

HANDLEY PAGE H.P.R. 7 DART HERALD

Manufacturer: Handley Page, Radlett, Great Britain
First flight: August 25, 1955
Number built: 50 (including 2 H.P.R. 3 Herald prototypes)
Wingspan: 94.75 ft.
Length: 75.5 ft.
Height: 24 ft.
Power plant: 2 Rolls-Royce Dart 527 turboprop engines
Cruise: approx. 267 mph
Range: approx. 1,118 miles
Crew: 2 in the cockpit, 1 in the cabin

BASED ON THE WRONG POWER PLANTS

In the early 1950s, the design team of the former Miles aircraft works in Reading, which was taken over by Handley Page in 1948, began planning one of the countless "DC-3 successors" of the time. The concept envisaged a high-wing aircraft powered by four conventional Alvis Leonides piston engines. Handley Page justified the decision not to use one of the turboprop engines that were already available at the time, such as the Rolls-Royce Dart engine, which powered the directly competing Fokker F-27 and Avro 748, by arguing the simpler maintainability of a piston engine at remote airfields that did not have an elaborate technical infrastructure.

The prototype with the registration G-AODE took off on its maiden flight on August 25, 1955. At that time, there were already twenty-nine orders in the sales books, which initially promised a bright future for this type of aircraft. However, it soon became apparent that the airlines were opting for the more advanced gas turbine engine. Further orders were therefore placed not with Handley Page but with Fokker in Amsterdam for its F-27 and for the Avro 748.

In 1958, Handley Page was forced to equip the two Herald prototypes with two Dart turboprops and named the aircraft Dart Herald in reference to the new turboprop engine from Rolls-Royce. Forty-eight production aircraft were produced in this form. These included four of the 100 series, with a maximum of fifty seats; thirty-six of the stretched 200 series for fifty-six passengers; and eight examples of the military 400 version, with a reinforced cabin floor and tail doors for easier loading and unloading of military equipment. The last flying Dart Herald, a 400 series operated by the British cargo and courier airline Channel Express with the registration G-BEYF, was retired in April 1999.

Handley Page and its Herald were no more successful than SAAB with its Scandia. The type's problems were homemade since initially four piston engines were used as propulsion until the potential of turboprops was recognized—too late. *Author's collection*

FOKKER F-27 FRIENDSHIP

Manufacturer: Fokker B.V., Amsterdam, the Netherlands
First flight: November 24, 1955
Number built: 581 (plus 206 FH 227s built under license
  in the United States)
Wingspan: 95 ft.
Length: 77 ft.
Height: 29.8 ft.
Power plant: 2 Rolls-Royce Dart Mk. 532-7 turboprop
  engines
Cruise: approx. 255 mph
Range: 1,150 mi.
Crew: 2 in the cockpit plus 2 in the cabin
Note: Data for the F-27 Mk. 600 operated by SAS

DUTCH BESTSELLER

Of the countless aircraft models that claimed to be a worthy successor to the legendary Douglas DC-3, the Fokker F-27 probably came closest to this goal. A total of 786 examples were built between 1955 and 1987 and flew for customers in sixty-three countries. The F-27 was the standard type on the short-haul routes of numerous airlines around the globe for decades.

Like so many turboprops of the 1950s, the Rolls-Royce Dart engine gave the Fokker F-27 the necessary speed, reliability, and economy. First installed in the Vickers Viscount, this indestructible standard engine was used in the HS 748 and Handley Page Herald, among others. However, neither British competitor came close to matching the success of the Dutch F-27.

Development of the F-27 dates back to 1950, when initial plans took shape under the designation P.275. On March 23, 1958, the first production aircraft destined for Ireland's Aer Lingus took off from Amsterdam—followed just a month later by the American version produced under license at Fairchild. The Fokker F-27 Mk. 100 became the basis for numerous further developed models with more-powerful engines, stretched fuselages, and modifications for special tasks. For the American market, in 1966, Fairchild developed the FH-227, whose fuselage was 6 feet longer than that of the F-27, in cooperation with Hiller. On both sides of the Atlantic, more and more civil and military variants of the basic design followed until production was discontinued in 1987, in favor of the likewise very successful successor model the Fokker F-50.

The only postwar aircraft that can claim to have inherited the mantle of the DC-3 to some extent is the Fokker F-27 Friendship, of which 586 were produced. *Author's collection*

AVRO / HAWKER SIDDELEY 748

Manufacturer: Avro / Hawker Siddeley, Woodford, Great Britain

First flight: June 24, 1960

Number built: 381

Wingspan: 98.5 ft.

Length: 67 ft.

Height: 24.8 ft.

Power plant: 2 Rolls-Royce Dart 532 turboprop engines

Cruise: approx. 248 mph

Range: 528 miles (max. payload)

Crew: 2 in the cockpit plus 2 in the cabin

Note: Data for 748-2A version

The Hawker Siddeley / British Aerospace 748 was a successful attempt by the British aviation industry to build a utility aircraft with superior capabilities in comparison to a DC-3. *Author's collection*

The design of this direct competitor of the Fokker F-27 goes back to A. V. Roe & Company Ltd., or Avro for short. When this company was absorbed by Hawker Siddeley in 1962, the successful British-built turboprop also changed its type designation from "Avro" to "HS" 748.

The launch customer, Skyways Coach-Air, operated its Avro 748s on the Channel route between Lympne in the UK and Beauvais in France from April 1962 onward. In addition to this small British airline, the Argentinean state airline Aerolíneas Argentinas was one of the first customers for this airliner powered by Rolls-Royce Dart turboprop engines. Eighteen Avro 748 Series 1s were built, and they were followed by the improved HS 748 Series 2, 2A, and 2B. In addition to the British final-assembly line,

HS 748s were also built under license at Hindustan Aeronautics Ltd. in Kanpur, India, for the Indian air force and for use by Indian Airlines. In Germany, seven HS 748s were used by the then Federal Air Traffic Control Agency (BFS) as survey aircraft for navigation facilities. In 1981, the German regional airline Deutsche Luftverkehrsgesellschaft (DLT) also put the first of six HS 748-2Bs into service. They flew under their own "DW" as well as "LH" flight numbers on behalf of Lufthansa in the 1980s. The HS 748s of today's Lufthansa City Line, which remained in the DLT fleet until 1989, initially wore a bright-red livery. When Lufthansa acquired a stake in DLT in 1985, its appearance was adapted to the more inconspicuous Lufthansa design.

In the early 1980s, the West German regional carrier DLT opted for this red paint scheme on its British Aerospace 748. The airline operated eight aircraft of this type: two leased 748-2A and six owned 748-2B. No other type in the DLT fleet received this striking red look. *Lufthansa*

CHAPTER 11
DC-1/DC-2/DC-3 SPECIFICATIONS

BBA Cargo was founded in 1946 as Brian & Brown Airfreighters. Until its bankruptcy in 1979, the Australian all-cargo airline operated three DC-3s. The photograph was taken on February 15, 1974, in Melbourne, Australia. *Tom Weihe*

Fiji Airways, founded in 1947 as the national airline of Fiji, was based at Nadi. This DC-3 with the registration VQ-FBF was photographed there on October 25, 1969, while being loaded. *Tom Weihe*

Photographer Tom Weihe captured this DC-3 of the Dutch airline Martinair at the airport of the Danish capital Copenhagen on November 27, 1966. *Tom Weihe*

Delta Air Transport was a Belgian airline that operated scheduled and charter flights out of Brussels on behalf of Sabena, among others. This aircraft, one of the airline's DC-3s, registration OO-CBU, visited Copenhagen-Kastrup Airport on September 6, 1969. *Tom Weihe*

The Norwegian airline Polaris Air Transport acquired this DC-3 with the registration LN-RTE from the regional airline Widerøe, also of Norway. This photograph was taken at Copenhagen Airport on June 16, 1966. *Tom Weihe*

Dakotas in service with South African Airways. *Transnet*

Meeting of two generations of aircraft: a DC-3 and the prototype of the Douglas DC-9. *SAS Museum, Oslo*

The Dutch airline KLM was a loyal Douglas customer and, in addition to the DC-2, also used the larger DC-3 and even the DC-5 on its route network. *Transnet*

A Douglas DC-6 and a DC-3 of the British operator Air Atlantique in formation flight. Both aircraft were still used commercially by the airline in the 1990s. *Air Atlantique*

Ramp scene at Zurich-Kloten Airport. Two Swissair DC-3s and an aircraft of the same type of the Swedish airline ABA. *Author's collection*

AB Aerotransport–Swedish Airlines began operating the DC-3 during the Second World War. Among other things, the aircraft were used to carry out dangerous courier flights between Sweden and Great Britain, during which two unarmed aircraft were lost together with their occupants after being shot down by German fighter aircraft. *SAS*

SPECIFICATIONS FOR THE DOUGLAS TWIN-ENGINED PROPELLER-DRIVEN AIRLINERS

DOUGLAS DC-1

Length	60.0 ft.
Wingspan	85.0 ft.
Height	16.0 ft.
Power plants	2 Wright Cyclone SGR-1820-F3 radial engines, each producing 690 hp
Empty weight	11,780 lbs.
Max. payload with 510 gallons of fuel	2,051 lbs.
Max. fuel	510 gallons
Gross weight	17,500 lbs.
Cruise	approx. 150 mph
Range	497 mi.
Capacity	12 passengers
Crew	2 in cockpit, 1 in the cabin

Source: Handbook of Operating Technique for the Douglas Transport Model DC-1, Douglas Aircraft Company

DOUGLAS DC-2

Length	62.0 ft.
Wingspan	85.0 ft.
Height	16.24 ft.
Power plants	2 Wright Cyclone SGR-1820-F3 radial engines, each producing 720 hp
Cruise	approx. 150 mph
Range	497 mi.
Capacity	14 passengers
Crew	2 in cockpit, 1 in the cabin
Range	497 mi.
Capacity	12 passengers
Crew	2 in cockpit, 1 in the cabin

Source: Swissair Version DC-2-115

DOUGLAS C-39 AND C-42

Length	61 ft., 6 in.
Wingspan	85.0 ft.
Height	18 ft., 8 in.
Power plants	C-39: 2 Wright Cyclone R-1820-55 radial engines, each producing 975 hp
	C-42: Wright R-1820-53 radial engines, each producing 1,000 hp
Cruise	C-39: 156 mph / C-42: 170 mph
Range	C-39: 1,170 mi. / C-42: 1,000 mi.
Cruise altitude	C-39: 20,600 ft. / C-42: 22,000 ft.
Crew	2 in cockpit

Source: Pilot's Operating Instructions, C-39 and C-42 Airplanes, Commanding General, Army Air Forces, March 25, 1941

DOUGLAS DST SKY SLEEPER

Length	64 ft., 4 in.
Wingspan	95 ft.
Height	16 ft., 11 in.
Wing area	987 sq. ft.
Power plants	2 Wright Cyclone G-2 / Pratt & Whitney Twin Wasp SB-G radial engines, each producing 1,000 hp
Empty weight	16,060 lbs. / 16,340 lbs.
Max. payload	7,940 lbs. / 7,660 lbs.
Max. gross weight	24,000 lbs. / 24,000 lbs.
Cruise (76% power)	192 mph / 194 mph
Cruising altitude	20,800 ft. / 22,100 ft.
Capacity	14 beds
Crew	2 or 3 in cockpit, 1 or 2 in the cabin

Source: The Douglas DST and DC-3, Douglas Aircraft Corporation

DOUGLAS DC-3

Length	64.5 ft.
Wingspan	95 ft.
Height	19.2 ft.
Wing area	987 sq. ft.
Power plants	2 Wright Cyclone G-102-A/2 radial engines, each producing 1,100 hp
Gross weight	25,133 lbs.
Cruise	approx. 174 mph
Range	540 mi.
Capacity	21 passengers
Crew	2 in the cockpit, 1 or 2 in cabin

Source: Swissair Version DC-3-227A

BASLER BT-67

Length	67.8 ft.
Wingspan	95.14 ft.
Power plants	2 Pratt & Whitney Canada PT6A-67R turboprops, each producing 1,281 hp
Fuel consumption	150.6 gal./hr.
Empty weight	18,298 lbs. (ski undercarriage 19,621 lbs.)
Gross weight	28,660 lbs.
Cruise	104 to 196 mph
Range empty	1,864 mi.
Range with 2,200 lb. payload	1,429 mi.

Source: Alfred Wegener Institute, Germany

BT-67 "Polar 6" of German Alfred-Wegener polar institute lands at the British Rothera Research Station in Antarctica. *Alfred-Wegener-Institut / Robert Ricker (CC-BY 4.0)*

BIBLIOGRAPHY

Davies, R. E. G. *Pan Am: An Airline and Its Aircraft*. Twickenham, UK: Hamlyn, 1987.

Provan, John. *Big Lift: Die Berliner Luftbruecke*. Bremen, Germany: Edition Temmen, 1998.

Yenne, Bill. *McDonnell Douglas: A Tale of Two Giants*. Greenwich, CT: Bison Books, 1985.

Contemporaneous documents, British European Airways.

Contemporaneous documents, Pan Am.

Contemporaneous documents, Scandinavian Airlines.

Contemporaneous documents, Swissair.

Visit of the restored Pan American World Airways "Clipper Tabitha May" at Paderborn Airport, Germany, on its Transatlantic Tour 2019. *Author's photo*

THE AUTHOR
WOLFGANG BORGMANN

Wolfgang Borgmann's enthusiasm for aviation was passed on to him by his parents, who were active in the aviation field. In his early years, he began building up an aviation historical collection that provides numerous rare photos and documents, as well as exciting background information, for his books. Since April 2000, Borgmann has been active as an author and, until February 2022, as a freelance aviation journalist. Since then he has worked as an editor for the leading German civil aviation magazine *Aero International*. He lives in Oerlinghausen, Germany. His website is www.aerojournalist.de.